'The story of the original Robinso[n] book that is as hypnotic and compell[ing] real subject. A great adventure story, a great read and a rea[d] for the art of biography.' Whitbread judging panel

'Authors without number have tried to repeat the success of Dava Sobel's elegant little book *Longitude*. I suspect that Diana Souhami may well have done it. *Selkirk's Island* is a delight from the moment the reader opens it ... But the real heart of this book, the memory that lingers most, is the island itself'

Christina Hardyment, *Independent*

'A swashbuckling yarn of booty and shipwreck ... forms the subject of Diana Souhami's new book. From storms and scurvy to salt pork and weevils, the chaotic shipboard life of the South Seas is brought pungently alive as the reader is press-ganged on to one of the notorious piratical expeditions of the early 18th century ... Souhami's account of Selkirk's voyage ... is masterful ... Souhami's description of Juan Fernandez is so evocative that I had half a mind to pack my bags to try to reach it' Giles Milton, *Sunday Times*

'Souhami ... is excellent on the grim, yet ever-hopeful lives of mariners in the eighteenth century, and gives a sharp picture of the exploits of privateers in the period, and the State's rapacious involvement' John Mullan, *Times Literary Supplement*

'Souhami begins with a lyrical introduction describing the natural beauties of the island; it is a paradisal episode, a moment out of time ... One of the pleasures of reading this book is the keen, lean freshness of the prose: the narrative zips along like a well-manned clipper' Greg Dart, *Guardian*

SELKIRK'S ISLAND

The scarlet shafts of sunrise — but no sail

Alfred, Lord Tennyson, *Enoch Arden* [†]

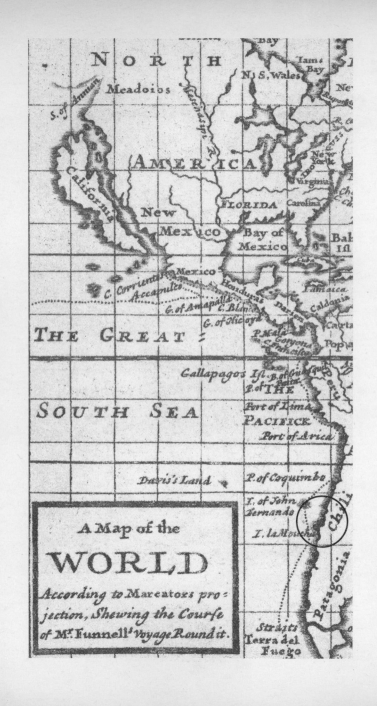

A Map of the
WORLD
According to Mercators pro-
jection, Shewing the Courfe
of Mr Funnell's voyage Round it.

DIANA SOUHAMI

Selkirk's Island

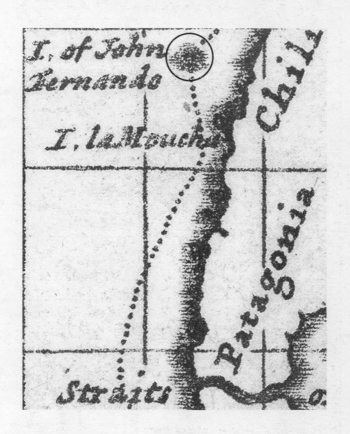

PHOENIX

A PHOENIX PAPERBACK

First published in Great Britain in 2001
by Weidenfeld & Nicolson
This paperback edition published in 2002
by Phoenix,
an imprint of Orion Books Ltd,
Orion House, 5 Upper St Martin's Lane,
London WC2H 9EA

A CIP catalogue record for this book
is available from the British Library.

ISBN 0 75381 334 3

Printed and bound in Great Britain by
The Guernsey Press Co. Ltd, Guernsey, C.I.

Design by Peter Campbell

TO MY MOTHER

ALL THANKS to Peter Campbell for his illumining design, to Rebecca Wilson at Weidenfeld for her publishing skills, and to my agent Georgina Capel for her acumen and watchful eye. Thanks, too, to Pat Chetwyn for copy editing the manuscript, and to Douglas Matthews, who compiled the index.

I am indebted to Peter LeFevre for rescuing me in the archives of the Public Record Office at Kew. He steered me through ships' logs, muster rolls, depositions, Letters of Marque and worse. And when I struggled with seemingly illegible manuscripts, he deciphered them with ease.

I have pillaged from the faultless scholarship of the maritime historian Glyn Williams, author of *The Great South Sea* and *The Prize of All the Oceans*. I am grateful for essential help to librarians at the Wellcome Institute, the Royal Geographical Society, the London Library, the British Library and the Natural History Museum, and to Brian Thynne, Curator of Hydrography at the National Maritime Museum, Greenwich, for making eighteenth-century charts and sailing directions available to me.

On the island I thank Pedro and Fabiana Niada for guided treks over impossible terrain, and for a memorable millennium-eve party; Manolo Chamorro for renting me a log cabin that looked out over the Pacific Ocean at the point where Selkirk was abandoned and rescued; Jaimie Sidirie who became my protector and translator; the painter Valeria Saltzman for her profound conversations; Ilke Paulentz for taking me on a terrifying journey in a small boat on Christmas Day to The Island's seal colonies; Ivan Leiva Silva at CONAF for explaining conservation issues to me; Oscar the chivalrous cook on the supply ship *Navarino* for looking after me on a two-day voyage to remote parts of the archipelago; Diamante at the Café Remo for cooking me so many fishes, and her husband for mixing those amazing *pisco* sours.

Back home, my deep thanks to Sheila Owen-Jones for rescuing me from the island when I felt powerless to leave, and for encouraging me through dark times as well as good. And once more and of course, for her unstinting kindness, my heartfelt thanks to Naomi Narod, my best friend for is it really thirty-four years.

Footnotes of passing interest are marked with an asterisk and appear on the text pages. References are marked with a dagger and appear as endnotes, beginning on page 219. Most of the engravings are taken from *A Voyage Round the World* by William Funnell (1707).

I

THE ISLAND

*The Island on which Alexander Selkirk was marooned,
for four solitary years, lies in the eastern Pacific Ocean
at latitude 34° south, three hundred and sixty miles
west of the coast of Chile. In 1966 the Chilean
government named it Robinson Crusoe Island, in tribute
to Selkirk, the real Robinson Crusoe, who inspired
Daniel Defoe to write his famous novel in 1719.*

*But Crusoe was a fiction and his island was a
fictional place. He and Selkirk, though both marooned,
as men were not alike. In imagining the reality of
Selkirk's abandonment, I have referred to his own scant
testimony, to that of his rescuers and fellow crewmen, to
contemporary eighteenth-century writers, and to
petitions from two women who each claimed to be his
wife. I have turned also to The Island whose storms and
daunting mountains evoke the ordeal of solitary
survival more forcefully than archives of inventories
and depositions, or the journals of privateers who
voyaged the world in wooden sailing ships in search of
gold.*

The Island of Juan Ferdenandos

Molten Stuff

DEFINED BY the vast South Sea, The Island from a wooden craft, far out, was a destination, a place of refuge. At first sight it looked no more than a grey blur. Plying the sea against strong tides and capricious winds, the blur turned to jagged mountains looming from the water. Dark clouds hung over the eastern end. They promised clear streams, meat, and respite from the journey's storms.

Ranging beneath the lee, searching for anchorage, the broken, craggy precipices revealed forests, cut by lush valleys, watered by cascades and streams. The bays of boulders and shingle became harbours of safety.

Spewed in the earth's heat, once The Island had been molten stuff beneath the earth's crust. Formed of columns of basalt, it was a causeway of mountain peaks, the highest, shaped like a huge anvil, rising three thousand feet above the ocean. Its rocks were grey, scoriaceous, slaggy, veined with olivine and picrite, coded with skeleton crystals of feldspar, aluminium, potash, lime… Its coast escarpments, high forested ridges and the dry seaward slopes of its valleys, were lava beds, relics from a magmatic flow: magma from the Greek 'to knead'. By its shores were lumps of black porous lava, like burnt-out clinker, like a dead fire.

The fire could rekindle. The Island changed with the scudding clouds, the waxing moon, a fall of rain. Sounds that cracked in echo round the mountains, warned of its awesome energy. Mariners told of the earth's explosion, of 'A Vulcan casting out Stones as big as a House', of a column that spouted from the sea filled with smoke and flames, of how the sea swept back in great rollers that left the bay dry, then surged in at such a height that trees uprooted and goats drowned.

Classifiers gave their views on geotectonic connections between The Island and the continent of South America and the movement of continental plates. They picked up pieces of rock, sailed home with them in boxes, identified the grains of colour these rocks contained as augite, magnetite and ilmenite and speculated on when the volcano had erupted and the manner in which time turns one thing into another. Their analyses made The Island less remote. If they named it, classified it, they could in a sense possess it and tame it to their will.

1702 *Mountains and Gorges*

IN THE SCHEME of things it was a chip of land – twelve miles long, four across, thirty-four miles round, four million years old. At the low parched western end only dwarf trees grew

(*Dendroseris litoralis* and *Rea pruinata*).* By a headland was a rocky bay, shaped like a horseshoe, where a small boat might land on sand and shingle.

The eastern cliffs rose sheer from the sea. Moss and algae grew where surf drained from the talus' edge. The sea under-mined the coastal wall and hollowed it as caves. Along the south-east shore were tufted grasses with high culms (*Stipa fernandeziana*). Waterfalls washed soil to the sea that stained the surf sepia. Beside a small bay, strewn with lava beds and furrowed by stony streams, two mountains rose, sculpted with hanging gullies carrying water after every rain.

Sea winds met the coast, rose high over the mountain crests, then cooled, condensed and fell as rain which drenched the ridges, gushed in torrents down the mountains, and in the lush green valleys turned to fast-flowing streams. Cloud shrouded the mountains while sunshine bathed the western hills. Winds gusted in the valleys in violent squalls. In the humid spring, rainbows arched the bays. Summer came in December and lasted until March.

In the forests that covered the mountain slopes were sweet-smelling sandalwood trees with dark brown bark, pimento with glossy leaves and pungent berries, large mayu trees with jutting roots, mountain palms with long straight trunks, dark green and ringed with scars. Trees uprooted in the squalling winds and thin mountain soil. In the gorges

*Classification of The Island's flora and fauna began in the nineteenth century. There were expeditions by a Scottish horticulturist, David Douglas, in 1824; an Italian botanist, Carlo Bertero, in 1830; a Chilean botanist, Federico Johow in the 1890s; a Swedish scientist, Carl Skottsberg in the early 1900s. It contin-ues with the work of a French botanist, Philippe Danton; a Chilean botanist, Clodomiro Marticorena.

rushes thrived with sword-shaped leaves and white flowers. *Gunnera masafuerae* spread parchment leaves. Tree ferns more than three feet tall, with dark green fronds grew in groves in the wooded valleys. Scandent ferns trailed over stones and fallen trunks. They clung to trees and branches. Bronze green filmy ferns filled the open glades, the banks of streams, the wet cliff walls.

Light-loving rosette trees grew on low rocks. Three times a year they flowered dark blue. Evergreen myrtles with white flowers graced the forest's edge, plum trees blossomed in spring. There was brushwood on the rock ledges and lichen on the stones. Luxuriant moss cushioned the boulders at the foot of the waterfalls. Colonies of flowering plants and grasses formed heathland. Herbs thrived by the valleys' streams.

In one valley of green pastures, cut by a fast-flowing stream there was a small harbour where boulders shifted under heavy swell. In calm seas a boat could land at the foot of a projecting rock, hollowed like a tunnel. The rock led to a cave sixteen feet above sea level. It was a place where a man might shelter.*

But only in one wide bay might a large ship find safe anchorage in deep water and its boats reach the shore. This bay was walled by high mountains cut by gulches. The grassland of its valley was screened by sandalwood trees and watered by streams. It was a place of echoes and fragrance: gentle at dawn and dusk, hostile in gusting wind. By its streams grew turnips and radishes, herbs, wild oats and grasses. Behind the valley

*It is called Selkirk's Cave, though he never sheltered in it, or stayed in the bay where it is, now named *Puerto Inglés*.

were high-walled gorges, dense with tree ferns and giant-leaved *Gunnera peltata*. From these gorges plunged waterfalls. Through thick forest a steep pass led to the south side of the island. At the summit of this pass, after an arduous climb, a man might scan the encircling sea. He would miss no ship that approached The Island. In time this summit became known as Selkirk's Lookout.

And beyond the valley and before it were ten thousand miles of ocean. The ocean was The Island's protection. It kept man (*Homo sapiens*) away. It carried only the daring or the desperate to its rugged, stony shore. Without intervention from man The Island found its times of burgeoning and times of repose.

Seals and Hummingbirds   1702

THE ISLAND served whatever life arrived on it by chance. If not one form then another. Gusting winds brought flies and bees. Plankton survived hurricanes. Spiders and the pupae of butterflies travelled unharmed in driftwood over vast stretches of ocean. Worms came in on the shoes of transient sailors, cats and rats sprang from anchored ships. There were forty-six kinds of mollusc and fifty sorts of fern.

A boa constrictor arrived coiled in the hollow of a cut tree. It had journeyed from Brazil for seven weeks over choppy seas. The tree washed ashore with the turning tide. The snake slithered over the stones of the bay and into the wooded valley. It found food – birds, seal pups, goats – shelter and sunshine, but no company. It sloughed its skin and danced alone.

Living things that reproduced without a partner colonised in a way the boa could not. Seeds survived the digestive tracts of thrushes, they stuck to the feet of albatrosses, they were carried from one part of The Island to another trapped in the fur of mice.

Fur seals (*Arctocephalus philippii*) with brown coats chose The Island for its stony bays, its deep water close to the shore and for the abundance of its fish. Agile in the sea, they dived and glided and lolled on their backs with folded flippers. On coastal boulders and islets they lumbered and wallowed in the sun. Their wet fur blended with the dark volcanic rocks. At times they appeared to weep. In November they came onshore to breed. Each mother gave birth to a single black-wool-covered pup.

There were huge sea lions (*Otaria jubata*) twenty feet long with furled snouts. In seasonal ritual to assert mastery they bellowed, fought and gored each other. Scars of sexual battle ringed their throats. The victor fathered a herd.

On every sea-washed rock, crabs scuttled. Beneath these rocks, lobsters grazed. They lived for decades and grew to three feet long. Pike shoaled at the sea's surface and at night seemed to fly, sand smelt spawned in seaweed, perch lurked near rocks for crabs, bacalao fish bred in deep water by the northern coast, bream scraped algae off the rocks with sharp teeth. There were cod and cavallies and blotched and spotted eels.

Goats came in on Spanish ships. Mariners released a few into the valley by the Great Bay, wanting meat when they careened their ships. The goats were small, dark brown, with curled horns and white marks on their foreheads and noses. They made for the hills and multiplied.

The Island was inhabited. It hosted, protected and sustained its guests. In the undergrowth in the valley were rats

(*Rattus rattus*), mice (*Mus musalus*), cats (*Felis domestica*). To all that holed up on it The Island offered sunlight, water, food and shelter. It gave the means of life.

The stars guided in birds. Hummingbirds with copper breasts and tiny pin-like beaks probed nectar from orange flowers. They wove hanging nests in the ferns. A bird that glistened like metal built its nest of moss in the fern groves and laid white eggs. Grey and white petrels swerved over the sea. Flycatchers darted in the valleys. Thousands of pairs of migrating puffins dug burrows in the cliffs. Two black-necked swans arrived, confused by a storm. They lived their life but did not breed.*

The Island was never quiet, never still. There was the chatter and whirr of hummingbirds, the barking of seals, the squealing of rats, the susurrus of waves, the wind in the trees. There were sounds of contentment, of killing and of casual disaster. A nocturnal seabird, the fardela, screamed in the night like a frightened child.

*It seems that birds are often marooned on The Island. In December 1999, when I was there, a storm-battered penguin was washed ashore, and a black swan, blown in on the wind from a lake south of Santiago, was escorted home by plane.

2

THE JOURNEY

The Jelly Fish.

Fig. 3.

Profits and Advantages   1703

SIX THOUSAND miles away, in London in a house in St James's Square, two men talked of gold. Thomas Estcourt, twenty-two, heir to his father's title, a gentleman of means, an entrepreneur, wanted to make a fortune.

William Dampier 'the Old Pyrateing Dog' was with him. He was thin with dark hair and eyes, thick brows and a slippery manner. Addicted to adventure, he had been a gunner in Sumatra, a logwood cutter in Mexico, a salvage merchant of Spanish wrecks off the American coast, a roving buccaneer. He had a wife, Judith, whom he seldom saw, a passion for sea travel and a recurring need for money.[†]

Dampier urged Estcourt to finance a booty-seeking voyage to South America. He promised him 'vast Profits and Advantages', riches beyond his dreams, if he would fund an armed and fitted ship and a fighting crew.[†]

Gold was the prize. He told Estcourt of the mines of Bahia,

Potosi, Santa Maria, of nuggets the size of hens' eggs, hacked from rocks with iron crowbars, of gold washed by rain from mountains into river beds.

This gold, he said, was all going to the Spaniards. They had a monopoly of the wealth of the South Sea lands and a stranglehold on its trade. 'They have Mines enough... more than they can well manage... they would lie like the *Dog in the Manger*; although not able to eat themselves, yet they would endeavour to hinder others.' They were an arrogant colonial power, despised by the indigenous people whom they exploited and abused. They had taken land and riches from them and made them into slaves.

Dampier put to Estcourt his plan to seize their treasure galleons and ransack the towns they occupied. He claimed they could not defend themselves: they had only three patrol ships to guard the coast from Chile to California. His ships would sail to Buenos Aires and capture the King of Spain's Treasure Fleet – two or three galleons bound for Spain loaded with mined gold. If that failed he would sail round Cape Horn, up the coast of Chile and attack the treasure galleons that regularly made for Callao, near Lima where the Spanish Viceroy resided. 'To this Port is brought all the Gold, Silver, Pearls, and Stones with Guineas and other Rich Things that the South part of the World Affords.'*

He would raid coastal towns of Chile, like Guayaquil,

*This quotation is from a compendium of charts and maps used by Dampier. The compendium was seized from a prize ship by a previous buccaneer, Bartholomew Sharp. It had been compiled by a Dutch cartographer, L.J. Waghenaer, in 1584. It was translated into English and copied by a London chartmaker, William Hack. There is a copy in the National Maritime Museum, London.

where houses and churches were filled with gold. And best of all, he would seize the prize of all the oceans – the great Spanish trading galleon that each June plied between Manila in the Philippines and Acapulco in Mexico.† Its voyage took six months.* It carried goods to the value of fourteen million Pieces of Eight from China, India, Persia, Japan.** It was laden with diamonds, rubies and sapphires from the East Indies, with spices and carpets from Persia, ivory from Cambodia, silks, muslins and calico from India, gold dust, tea, porcelain and furniture from China and Japan. Its cargo was of 'prodigious Value'. When it arrived in Acapulco a market was held which lasted thirty days. Its riches were carried by ship to Peru and by mule train across Mexico to Vera Cruz, then Europe.***

On its return to Manila the galleon was loaded with gold and silver coin and plate. It was the 'most desirable Prize that was to be met with in any part of the Globe'. Only once had an English ship taken it, in 1587 in a battle that lasted six hours. The captain Thomas Cavendish and his crew returned home as heroes. When they sailed in triumph up the Thames they flew a standard of blue and gold silk and hoisted sails of blue damask. Each sailor wore a gold chain round his neck. Queen Elizabeth greeted them at Greenwich.

Such was the pride of conquest. If the Acapulco galleon could be taken, or even with a lesser prize, Estcourt's fortune

---

* The gender of ships is by convention female. But I am not familiar enough with a ship to call it her or she.

** Pieces of Eight, the parlance of pirates, were Spanish dollars or 'piastre' (pieza de ocho).

*** It was known as both the Acapulco and the Manila galleon. It took the name of its port of departure.

was assured. This was more than a crude raid for plunder. To be a privateer was qualitatively different from being a bucca-neer, pirate or Mere Theaf. Here was a patriotic venture in the service of Queen Anne. England, in alliance with Austria and Holland, was at war with Spain and France. Royal Proclama-tion legitimised 'Reprisal against the sea-borne property of Their Catholic Majesties, the Kings of France and Spain'. The High Court of Admiralty would grant a licence, a 'letter of Marque', for this assault on the enemy which coincid-entally would make its perpetrators rich.

Estcourt, though nervous of the heavy cost of failure, was seduced. He paid for the *Nazareth*, a ship of about 200 tons, spent four thousand pounds to have it fitted out as a privateer, renamed it the *St George* and engaged William Dampier as its captain.*

1698 *A Daring Man*

DAMPIER KNEW well the risks and rewards of his proposed adventure. More, as he put it, 'than a Carrier who jogs on to his Inn without ever going out of his Road'. For thirteen years, in a series of voyages, he had circumnavigated the world. He had sailed cruel seas in wooden ships called *Loyal Merchant*, *Defence*, *Revenge*, *Trinity* and *Batchelor's Delight*. He had survived storms, torture, shipwreck, mutiny, gun-battles, disease and near-starvation. 'Hardened to many

---

*A ship is a large, sea-going vessel, as opposed to a boat. A galleon is a ship of war. A pinnace is a light vessel attendant on a larger one. A bark is a small sail-ing vessel.

Fatigues', inured to rough living, he called himself 'a daring man, such as would not be easily baffled'.†

An experienced pilot and navigator of the South Sea, it was proof of his cunning that the Spaniards feared his name. He was a strategic thief, an able chronicler of what he saw, and a store of information. He interrogated prisoners: how many families were in their town, what guns, lookouts, small arms and sentinels did they have, were they 'Copper-colour'd as Malattoes, Musteseos or Indians', were they rich, what did their riches consist of, what were the chief manufactures of the region, where was the best landing, was there a river or creek nearby, could the area be attacked without notice...

He always took the Pilot-books of ships he captured. 'These we found by Experience to be very good Guides' and he charted the 'Trade Winds, Breezes, Storms, Seasons of the Year, Tides and Currents'.

In all my Cruisings among the Privateers, I took notice of the risings of the Tides; because by knowing it, I always knew where we might best haul ashore and clean our ships.

He kept journals of his Cruisings and in 1697 an edited version of these, *A New Voyage Round the World*, went into four editions. Its title-page lured with the scope of his travels:

the *Isthmus of America*, several Coasts and islands in the *West Indies*, the Isles of *Cape Verd*, the Passage by *Terra del Fuego*, the *South Sea* Coasts of *Chile* and other *Philippine* and *East-India* Islands near *Cambodia*, *China*, *Formosa*, *Luconia*, *Celebes*, &c. *New Holland*, *Sumatra*, *Nicobar* Isles; the *Cape of Good Hope*, and *Santa Helena*.

Here were undreamed-of places, journeys of wonder and terror, beyond the reach of most. Safe in their Armed chairs, Dampier's readers might brave a tornado in a canoe 'ready to be swallowed by very foaming Billow', survive storms that 'drenched us all like so many drowned Rats', hear how undrowned rats aboard ship ate the stores of maize, how men died of scurvy and 'malignant fever', got eaten by sharks, attacked by snakes and murdered by the Spaniards 'stripped and so cut and mangled that You scarce knew one Man'.

Dampier offered his readers quotidian detail, casual cruelty and wild adventure. Plunder was the goal, but he was a keen observer. He interspersed his accounts of pillage and arson with lessons in ethnography, anthropology, hydrography and natural history. He described the anatomy and behaviour of a shark and drew its picture, before advising how to eat it: boiled, squeezed dry, then stewed with vinegar and pepper. The guanos of the Galapagos Islands were 'so tame that a Man may knock down twenty in an Hour's Time with a Club'. Giant tortoises were fat and sweet to eat and stayed semi-alive and edible for days if turned on their backs. Turtle doves were so trusting 'that a Man may kill 5 or 6 dozen in a Forenoon with a Stick'.

Dampier had eaten monkeys, penguins, locusts and anything that moved. Flamingoes, he wrote, made

very good Meat, tasting neither fishy nor in any way unsavoury. Their tongues are large, having a large Knob of Fat at the Root, which is an excellent Bit, a Dish of Flamingoes Tongues being fit for a Prince's Table.

His readers might learn the practicalities of careening a ship, or of mending sails, the logistics of finding a harbour or of ransacking a town. He told them of the symptoms of scurvy, the supposed influence of the moon on tides and how in a storm to furl the mainsail and ballast the mizzen. He wrote of sago trees, of vanilla pods drying in the sun, of antidotes for the stings of scorpions, of the Natives of Guam 'ingenious beyond any other People in making Boats or Proas' so swift and streamlined they could travel at twenty-four miles an hour, of war dances and pageants that celebrated the circumcision of eleven-year-old boys on the island of Mindanao: 'The Mahometan Priest takes hold of the Fore-skin with two Sticks and with a pair of Scissors snips it off.'

Dampier was circumspect about sex. For the more refined of his crew it was barter. They had their Delilahs or Black Misses, hired for a trinket or a silver wrist band. More often it was rape, unwanted offspring and abandonment. Tawny-coloured children of uncertain English paternity, were born on board ship to black slaves. At Mindanao, where 'the Natives are very expert at Poisoning', two sailors were murdered when they 'gave Offence through their general Rogueries and by dallying too familiarly with Women'. The ship's surgeon dissected their corpses and revealed livers as black as cork.

For all their scandal and revelation, Dampier's journals were selective. In England he courted acceptance in respectable circles. Piracy was punished on the gallows. He did not want it broadcast that he had assisted in mutiny, kept company with rogues, connived at the rape of women and the abuse of prisoners. In the Chancery Courts in London, down the years, testimony accrued against him for being indecisive, capricious, heedless of consultation and cruel.

A 'vexatious' voyage under his captaincy, in 1698, in the *Roebuck* to 'ye remoter part of the *East India Islands* and the neighbouring Coast of *Terra Australis*' concluded with the mutiny of his crew, the sinking of the ship, a court martial on his return to England and the verdict of the Court that 'the said Captain Dampier is not a Fitt person to be Employ'd as commander of any of her Majesty's ships.'[†]

In particular he was found guilty of 'very Hard and cruell usage' towards his first lieutenant George Fisher. He had belaboured him with a stick, confined him in irons 'for a considerable time', imprisoned him on shore 'in a strange Countrey', then sent him home. By way of justification, Dampier claimed that Fisher railed at him for hours, 'shaked his Fist att me, Grind in my Face, and told me that he cared not — for me... called me Old Dog, Old Villain, and told my men, Gents take care of that Old Pyrateing Dog for he designs to Run away with you and the King's Ship.'[†]

Such altercations were not included in Dampier's edited *A New Voyage Round the World*. He admitted to receiving editorial help. It was, he said, 'far from being a Diminution to one of my Education and Employment, to have what I write, Revised and Corrected by Friends.' He catered to refined readers and dedicated the book to Charles Montagu, President of the Royal Society and First Lord of the Treasury. It mattered to him to be invited to dine with the diarists Samuel Pepys and John Evelyn and the satirist, Jonathan Swift, and to be on terms with the writer and political advisor, Daniel Defoe and the First Lord of the Admiralty, the Earl of Orford.

1691   *Giolo of Meangis*

ONE OF Dampier's lurid business ventures concerned Giolo, a prince from the royal family of Meangis, a small fishing island off New Guinea.[†] Giolo was a much tattooed man. A wife had covered him with maps and patterns – all over his chest, shoulders, thighs, back, arms and legs. She had pricked his skin then rubbed in pigments from the resin of plants.

She did him a disservice in making him so conspicuous. Tattoos were uncommon in England apart from crucifixes on forearms. Giolo was captured by booty seekers and taken from his island. He was a curiosity, a marketable commodity. Dampier bought him in Madras in 1690 from a Mr Moody, then took him home, expecting to gain 'no small Advantage to myself from my painted Prince'. He planned to exhibit Giolo for a fee to intrigued spectators and use him to impress affluent businessmen to put up cash for another venture. Giolo, he claimed, had told him

that there was much Gold on his Iland, and I know he could not be inform'd of the manner of gathering it unless he had known it himselfe besides, he knew not the value of it neither have the people of his Iland any comerce with other People but what induced me to believe that there is Gold on his Iland is because all the Ilande near doe gather gold more or less therefore why should this be without.[†]

Dampier knew the gold's value. With Giolo's guidance he would gather it. He would trade in spices too, for there were cloves and nutmegs on Meangis.

Giolo sailed for England with Dampier in the *Defence*. He arrived in London in September 1691 his health broken by misery and the ship's diet of salt meat and tainted water. His dream was to return home to his small, sunny island. Dampier's enthusiasm for him faded when he gained scant financial advantage from him. He found him a burden to feed and house, so he sold him. Giolo's new owners advertised him in a printed broadsheet:

This admirable Person is about the Age of Thirty, graceful, and well pro-
portioned in all his Limbs, extreamly modest and civil, neat and cleanly;
but his Language is not understood, neither can he speak English.

He will be exposed to publick view every day (during his stay in
Town)... at his Lodgings at the *Blew Boars-head* in *Fleetstreet*, near *Water-
Lane*: Where he will continue for some time, if his health will permit.

But if any Persons of Quality, Gentlemen or Ladies, do desire to see
this noble Person, at their own Houses, or any other convenient place, in
or about this City of *London*, they are desired to send timely notice and he
will be ready to wait upon them in a Coach or Chair, any time they please
to appoint, if in the daytime.[†]

Captive and marooned, Giolo lost hope of rescue, of
returning home. His new owners tried to make him more of
a feature. They advertised that on his back, to be viewed for a
fee, was 'a lively Representation of one quarter part of the
World while the Arctick and Tropick Circles center in the
North Pole on his Neck'. Etched on one miserable man was
the unmet world. His tattoos, they claimed, made him
immune to 'all sorts of the most venomous, pernicious Creatures ...; such as Snakes, Scorpions, Vipers and Centapees
&c.'[†]

They displayed him too, for sixpence a peek, at market
sideshows along with other wonders of nature: dwarfs, giants,
dancing bears, hermaphrodites from Angola, two female
children joined at the crown of their heads, a child covered in
fish scales, and Jane Paterson of Northumberland who gave
birth to a monster with the head, mane and hooves of a horse
and the body of a boy.

Giolo's career as a freak was not happy nor his immunity
to poison sure. He caught smallpox which made him tear at his
tattooed skin. He scratched himself to death in Oxford.

A Man Named Will

DAMPIER KNEW of The Island, how fecund it was and re-mote. It was not owned or claimed by any monarch. Booty seekers who roamed the South Sea could, if they found it, use it to careen their ships.

It was Christmas Day 1680 when he first reached it. He was with a gang of buccaneers led by Captain Bartholomew Sharp, 'a Man of an undaunted courage not fearing in the least to look an insulting Enemy in the face'.[†] They had been at sea the best part of a year, had endured storms and torrential rains, scurvy and fever, and seen most of their crew murdered. A prize, a ship loaded with three hundredweight of gold, had escaped them. They were bedraggled, dispirited and ill. They wanted fresh meat, greens, clean water and dry land.

A prisoner, a Spanish pilot, guided their ship, the *Trinity*, to the north-west bay near the hollowed rock and the cave. The bay offered no protection. They faced rocks dashed by high waves. Twice they lost their moorings in heavy swell and shifting boulders. They could see a grove of sandalwood trees, a clear stream, and goats in the mountains, but no place for a boat to land. They moved east to the Great Bay with the wide valley. The shore seemed to belong to the fur seals 'the like of which I have not taken notice of anywhere but in these seas' Dampier wrote. There were thousands of them

I might say possibly Millions, either sitting on the Bays, or coming and going in the Sea round The Island... They lie at the Top of the Water, Playing and Sunning themselves for a Mile or Two from the Shore. When they come out of the Sea they bleat like Sheep for their Young; and though they pass through Hundreds of other Young Ones before they come to their own, yet they will not suffer any of them to suck. The Young Ones are like Puppies and lie much Ashore, but when Beaten by any of us, they, as well as the Old Ones will make towards the Sea and swim very swiftly and nimbly. On Shore, however, they lie very sluggishly and will not go out of our ways unless we Beat them but Snap at us. A Blow on the Nose soon Kills them.[†]

There were plenty of Blows on the Noses. Such blows were sport and afforded pleasure. These creatures were there to be killed. Fur skins were wearable, seal meat edible, blubber was suitable for frying food and for lantern oil. Once there was nemesis. As a sailor skinned a young sea lion he had clubbed to death its mother came up unperceived:

getting his head in her mouth she with her teeth scored his skull in notches in many places, and thereby wounded him so desperately that, though all possible care was taken of him, he died in a few days.[*]

Christmas on The Island in 1680 was not tranquil for the buccaneers. It was summer but the weather was stormy and the men mutinous. They had gambled away their plunder, now 'scarce worth a groat'. They blamed their captains for the failure of the voyage. They turned out Sharp, elected John Watling an 'old privateer and stout seaman', to replace him, and put Edmund Cook in leg irons when his servant, William, 'confessed that his master had often buggered him'.[†]

A fortnight later three Spanish warships headed in to The Island. In their haste to be gone the buccaneers abandoned a Miskito Indian,[**] a slave, a man of no consequence to them

* This record of nemesis quoted in George Anson, *A Voyage Round the World* (1748) is later than my story. Perhaps seals wreaked vengeance more than once.
** Miskitos are South American Indian people from the Atlantic coast of what is now Nicaragua and Honduras.

named Will. Will was in the mountains hunting goats. From high above the Great Bay he saw the *Trinity* departing and the Spaniards approaching.

Will was one of any number of the marooned, but he fared better than Watling who within a month was killed in a sea skirmish. He went high into the mountains to evade capture by the Spaniards. He had with him a gun and a knife. When his powder ran out he notched the knife blade and sawed the iron gun barrel into pieces. Using his gun flint to spark fire, he hammered and bent the molten iron with stones to forge harpoons, lances, fishing hooks and a blade. 'By long labour' he ground these tools into shape.

Out of stone he honed a ten-inch double-bladed hatchet and bored a hole in the middle for a wooden handle. Among the trees, by a stream near the sea he built a wooden hut. He spread his bed with goatskins and cut sealskin into fishing lines.

For three years Will survived alone. In 1684 Dampier was again cruising in the South Sea. On 22 March from high in the forest, Will watched Dampier's ship, the *Batchelor's Delight* approach The Island. Knowing the crew would crave fresh food he cudgelled three goats and roasted them on stones with cabbages and herbs. He waited on the rocks as the men came ashore by canoe. Dampier described the encounter:

When we landed a Meskito Indian named Robin, first leap'd ashore and running to his Brother Meskito Man, threw himself flat on his face at his feet, who helping him up, and embracing him, fell flat with his face on the Ground at Robin's feet, and was by him taken up also.

We stood with pleasure to behold the surprize and tenderness and solemnity of this Interview, which was exceedingly affectionate on both sides; and when their Ceremonies of Civility were over, we also that stood gazing at them drew near, each of us embracing him we had found here, who was overjoyed to see so many of his old Friends come hither, as he thought purposely to fetch him.

He was named Will, as the other was Robin. These were names given them by the English, for they had no Names among themselves; and they take it as a great favour to be named by any of us; and will complain for want of it, if we do not appoint them some name when they are with us: saying of themselves they are poor Men, and have no Name.[†]

1574-91 Juan Fernandez

A MERCHANT SEAMAN gave The Island a name. Don Juan Fernandez sailed from Peru to Chile in October 1574 in his ship *Nuestra Senora de los Remedios*.* The accepted route down the coast from Callao to Valparaiso was unpredictable. It could take three months or a year. Strong currents and headwinds made the going hard and slow.

Juan Fernandez sailed west to the open sea to try for better speed. After twenty-six days he chanced on The Island. It was one of two, a little archipelago. At its southern tip across a strait of turbulent water, was a satellite islet, a bare rock, five and a half miles in circumference. Ninety miles west its sister island rose from the sea to a height of five thousand feet. He glimpsed its gorge, its canyon walls, its waterfalls.

He called the bigger island *Mas a Tiera* (Nearer Land), its satellite *Santa Clara*, the western island *Mas a Fuera* (Further Away). Collectively he called them the islands of *Santa Cecilia* for the 22 November, when he first saw them, was her feast day.** Others called them the islands of *Juan Fernandez* for it

*Our Lady of Refuge.   **St Cecilia was the patron saint of music. She was beheaded in AD 230 for refusing to worship idols.

was he who had been blown near to them, had 'discovered' them. Thus they were in some sense his.

He sailed due east and reached Valparaiso in four days. No one believed his claim to have made the voyage from Lima in only a month. He was accused of using sorcery to pervert the winds and tides and was interrogated by officers of the Inquisition. When other mariners proved his route he was rewarded with a country estate at Quillota for service to the King of Spain and given the title Chief Pilot of the South Sea.

Merchants then went to The Island to fell its sandalwood trees and to kill fur seals and trap lobsters. Plans were mooted to colonise it, to use it as a base to defend the South Sea which the Spaniards viewed as theirs. A businessman, Captain Sebastian Garcia Carreto of Estremadura shipped lobsters, timber and sealskins back to the port of Valparaiso. Through this enterprise The Island became in some sense his. Don Alonso de Sotomayor, Governor of Santiago, Captain General and Chief Justice of the Kingdom of Chile issued him with a land grant on 20 August 1591:

in the name of His Majesty, by virtue of the Royal Order which authorizes me to grant Lands, I concede to you Five Hundred *cuadras* of Land on the said Island ... I commission you to take possession of the Land which I in the name of His Majesty grant to you, so that you make them yours with all their Fruits and Advantages.[†]

Captain Carreto stocked The Island with goats, pigs, turnips and sixty South American Indians. The Indians felled trees, built boats and huts, grew crops, caught fish and lobsters and served his business plan. They observed the rainbow that arched the valley in the morning mist, heard the call of the fardelas, saw the hummingbirds drinking the nectar of flowers. Only for a time was The Island their home. Home was where they were taken to or was a place denied.

Carreto's colony failed. It was locked in the great valley in the northern bay. The Island was too remote from the mainland for business to succeed. He tired of the enterprise. The Indians left traces: abandoned huts and crude paths through the deep forest. When they left, the goats scampered high into the mountains, the crops grew wild, the seals and fishes thrived. Only occasionally did small ships ply from Valparaiso to plunder cargoes of wood, fish and fur. And only occasionally did mariners such as Dampier arrive to careen their ships, sow 'Garden Seeds for Salading' and replenish their supplies.

1703 *The* St George *and the* Cinque Ports

THOMAS ESTCOURT, with three other backers, drew up Articles of Agreement for the South Sea voyage of the *St George*. These were to be the defining rules of the enterprise – a guide to order, the accepted reference for settling disputes.

'No purchase, no pay' were the terms of engagement for officers and crew. It was an inducement to fight, if plunder was the only reward. A Council of Ships' Officers would regularly review progress of the expedition. Records were to be made of meetings and of resolutions passed. Meticulous account books were to be kept of all cargoes seized.

Dampier was to try, in the course of the voyage, to get plunder back to the owners – to avoid losing it in shipwreck or attack. On his return to London, spoils would be meted out in the time-honoured division between bosses and workers –

two thirds for the four owners, one third for the one hundred and twenty officers and crew in shares according to rank. A fifth of the total booty would go to the Crown. During the voyage, to buy bits and pieces – liquor, sex, parrots – each man might claim one share of his total entitlement.

Dampier refused to sail without Edward Morgan, pirate, thief and his ally on a previous buccaneering expedition. Departure was delayed until Morgan was released from prison on a sentence for fraud. He was then hired as 'Purser and Agent', accountable for all expenditure. Another friend, John Ballett, was to go as Surgeon and James Barnaby who had sailed with Dampier in the *Roebuck* was to go as Second Lieutenant. John Clipperton was Chief Mate, William Funnell Second Mate, James Hill Master, and Samuel Huxford First Lieutenant.

It was agreed that none of the crew was to be marooned or put ashore in the course of the voyage. The *St George* would sail in consort with a sister ship the *Fame* commanded by Captain Pulling. Dampier put up two thousand pounds surety for the 'civil and honest behaviour of officers and men'. He accepted he would be fined five thousand pounds if he failed 'diligently and faithfully to observe perform fulfill accomplish and keep all and every one of the said Articles'.†

He assured an income for his wife Judith while gone for what might be years. During the setting up of this voyage, in 1702, he worked as 'an Extraordinary Land-carriage Man in ye Port of London', transporting ships' cargo to its destination. He appealed to Lord Godolphin at the Treasury to guarantee his wage from this. Godolphin issued a Warrant in January 1703:

William Dampier is Ordered to Sea for some time upon publique Service and hath therefore prayed that his Sallary in ye mean time may be continued and paid to his Assigns, Which Request I think Reasonable and do therefore Authorize and Require you to cause the Sallary of the said William Dampier to be continued for him on ye Establishment and paid to his Asses during his absence occasioned by ye particular Service upon which he is now sent.[†]

Thus Dampier's respectability. On 16 April the *London Gazette* announced that 'Captain William Dampier, being prepared to depart on another Voyage to the West Indies had the Honour to Kiss her Majesty's Hand, being introduced by His Royal Highness the Lord High Admiral'.[†]

The *St George* was victualled for eight months, had two sets of sails, five anchors, five cables, a ton of spare cordage, twenty-two cannons, one hundred small arms, thirty cutlasses, thirty barrels of gunpowder, thirty rounds of great shot and a ton of small shot. With one hundred and twenty men, it was deliberately overcrewed. For its size twenty men would have been enough. There was only twenty-five feet of living space in the bows. But extra men were needed to crew captured ships and ransack towns, and the expectation was for many to die, to be killed fighting or to desert.

The prospect was of hardship and danger. All ports of the South Sea were closed to these men. They could freely anchor only at small islands unclaimed by Spain. If captured they would be killed, left to starve, or holed up in a Spanish prison. Prizes were elusive. The chance of contracting scurvy or the bloody flux was greater than of acquiring gold. Violence and mutiny were always close. The crew was comprised of the disaffected and desperate of any nationality or age. Thoughts of booty and quantities of free liquor were their enticement.

And perhaps too the wide sea, the night sky, adventure, unknown lands and departure from a no-hope life.

Before leaving London, Dampier and Captain Pulling quarrelled. Pulling then refused to sail in consort with Dampier and instead went off to 'cruize among the Canary-Islands'. (His ship blew up in Bermuda in August 1703 when a man drew brandy from a barrel with a lighted candle in his hand.)

Pilot ships guided the *St George* down the Thames, across the Flats and into the Downs, the anchorage at Kent near the Goodwin Sands. A fair wind took the ship into the Channel on 30 April 1703. Eighteen days later it reached Kinsale, a walled market town in Cork in southern Ireland. There was a sandy cove, the Swallow, dry at low water, the ruins of an old fort, deep water in the bay of Money Point and rocks called 'the Sovereign's Bollocks' to be avoided, 'they are very foul'.

For five months the *St George* lingered in Kinsale harbour waiting for a replacement consort, the *Cinque Ports Galley*. The men got bored. Dampier put ashore those he thought useless, and took on new recruits. Supplies dwindled and the ship was revictualled. The staple diet was bread, meat, cheese and a gallon of beer a day per man. Beer was brewed extra strong to keep better. There were kegs, demijohns, bottles, hogsheads and casks of rum, claret, brandy and arak.* Water, unsafe to drink and used only for cooking, formed the ground tier of casks in the hold and served as ballast.

Meat was thought the basis of a healthy diet and it travelled live – as many caged and tethered bullocks, sheep, pigs, goats, hens and geese as could be crammed in. There was a stench of

---

*Dampier, in *A New Voyage* (1697), explained that 'Arack is distill'd from Rice, and other things.'

excrement and animal misery. Cats were carried to kill the ships' rats, and dogs to hunt on land. Salt beef and pork were supposed to hold good for up to five years. The meat was salted twice with Newcastle white and French bay salt and packed in casks filled with 'bloody pickle' made by boiling, scumming and clarifying the meat juices. Casks of butter and Suffolk cheese – hard and thin and made from skimmed milk – were supposed to last six months. There were supplies of biscuits, dried peas, currants, rice and oatmeal and plenty of tobacco for chewing, but no citrus fruits or greens.[†]

Even before leaving Kinsale the relationship between Dampier and his backers soured. The owners complained about the delays and Dampier's frequent requests for money – he wanted further refitting of the ship and an advance of £450. They were dismayed, too, at the amount of beer the crew consumed: 'more than a hogshead every day and everything seems to be managed with the same sort of husbandry'. The owners' agents wrote that they had 'so ill an opinion of Captain Dampier's conduct and management that we begin to despair of the voyage and advise you to give over for lost what you have already laid out'.[†]

The *Cinque Ports Galley* arrived on 6 August. It was a small ship of about 130 tons, mounted with 20 guns and carrying 90 men.[†] Charles Pickering, its Captain and part-owner, had earlier sailed in it to Marseilles 'to aid the Queen's enemies'. He, too, had spent considerable time in Court on charges of treachery, evasion of Customs and fraud. Among his officers were Thomas Stradling his First Lieutenant; Thomas Jones, Mate; John Cobham, Gunner; James Broady, Surgeon; and a dour Scot, Alexander Selkirk, who was the ship's Master.[†]

Selkirk or Selcraig

OFFICIALS VARIOUSLY spelled his name Selcraig, Selchraige, Sillcrigge, Silkirk, Selkirk. He was born in 1680 in Nether Largo in Fife in Eastern Scotland, in one of a huddle of houses that faced the wide curve of Largo Bay.* A long beach linked the neighbouring towns of Ely and Anstruther. Fishing and merchant ships anchored in Largo harbour and sometimes warships seeking crews for voyages to distant seas. Behind the bay was a dense woodland called Keil's Den. In the mouth of the Firth of Forth was the Isle of May, inhabited by seals, and colonies of breeding puffins, cormorants, kittiwakes and terns.

Alexander was the seventh and last son of John Selcraig and his wife Euphan. They had no daughters and had been married thirteen years when he was born. His father expected him to work in the family trade: scraping, stretching and tanning hides and cobbling them into shoes. For Alexander the sea promised adventure, gold and escape from small-town life. His mother thought because he was the seventh son he was destined to bring luck to others and fortune to himself. She encouraged his ambition, which was 'the cause of much domestic strife and bickering'.†

The Selcraigs were Scottish Presbyterians, contemptuous of England as a colonising power. There was one monarch but there were two economies. A Settlement in 1689 took

---

*According to his own testimony, in a Deposition now lodged in the Public Record Office, London (C24/1321 pt.1), Selkirk's year of birth was 1680. (See page 182). In biographical reference to him, and on plaques and statues to his memory, the date given is 1676.

Scotland's constitution of Church and State closer to England. Protesters 'exprest their Inveteracy with Stones and Dirt and Curses'. The 'hot Presbyterians' and 'Squadroni', as Daniel Defoe called them, broke windows, 'went Hallowing in the Dark and called the English Dogs.' They beat drums, armed themselves with pistols, swords and daggers and declared that all Scotland should stand together and there would be no Union.[†]

In Glasgow ringleaders were locked up in the Castle. In Dumfries, the offending Settlement was burned at the Market Cross. In Nether Largo, Alexander's eldest brother John led 'a great mob, armed with staves and bludgeons' who barred the church door, jeered at the Episcopalian minister, John Auchinleck, for being anglicised and a traitor and threatened to kill him if he held the Sunday service. Auchinleck got away fast. He 'divided what Money there was amongst the Poor and retired from his Charge'.

Six years later, aged fifteen, Alexander was accused of 'undecent beaiviar' in the same church. He was summoned to appear before a disciplinary session of its Elders. The parish records read:

1695. *Alexander Selchraig to be summoned August, 25*. This same day the Session mett. Alexr. Selchraig, Son to John Selchraig, Elder, in Nether Largo, was dilated for his Undecent Beaiviar in ye Church; the Church Officer is ordirred to ga and cite him to compear befoor our Session agst ye nixt dyett.

August, 27th ye Session mett. Alexr. Selchraig, Son to John Selchraig, Elder, in Nether Largo, called but did not compear, being gone avay to ye Seas; this Business is continued till his return.[†]

New Caledonia

AWAY AT ye seas for eight years, from the time of his indictment by the Largo Elders to when he joined the *Cinque Ports* as Master, Selkirk became a hardened man and mariner. Chances are he learned his skills, aged fifteen on, in a Scottish expedition to the South Sea. It was Scotland's assertion as a colonial power. It became known as the Darien Disaster.[†]

The intention was to set up a colony on the Isthmus of Darien, a bleak strip of land in north Panama between the Caribbean and South Seas. This 'little Caledonia' was to control an overland trade route that would channel the wealth of the world, east and west, to Scotland.

William Paterson was the driving force behind the scheme: in 1695 he founded the Company of Scotland, trading to Africa and the Indies. He described the Isthmus of Darien as 'this door of the seas, and the key to the universe'.[†] He was much influenced by Lionel Wafer, a shipmate of Dampier's, on the *Trinity* in 1684. Buccaneer, surgeon and barber, Wafer kept a journal of his travels to Panama. Dampier made a transcript of this which he gave to Paterson to read. Wafer wrote of the gold mines of Canea and Santa Maria and the road to Portobello, used by muletrains loaded with the wealth of Peru. He was lyrical about Darien, its valleys watered with perennial springs, its fertile soil and pineapples as big as a man's head.

The indigenous Cuna Indians would welcome the colonisers, Wafer said. Copper-skinned and adorned with rings and plates of gold, they lived in simple villages in huts roofed with plantain leaves. They hated the Spaniards who had made them into slaves. Wafer, though, was accepted because he cured them with 'Physic and Phlebotomy'. In return they told him about their land.

Grand plans were made. Twenty per cent of taxes and profits from merchandise, gold, silver and jewels, would go to the Company of Scotland. The colony would be divided into districts run by councillors – Fort St Andrew, on a promontory guarding the bay, New Edinburgh, nestling in the mountains.

Five ships were prepared: the *Caledonia*, *St Andrew*, *Unicorn*, *Dolphin* and *Endeavour*. Recruitment advertisements posted in Scottish coffee houses promised volunteers like Selkirk adventure and riches. Each man would get fifty acres of agricultural land and a house in fifty square feet of ground. Councillors would have twice that. Relatives would be shipped out at the Company's expense.

Opposition came from the Lords of Trade and Plantations in London. They aimed to halt the scheme and annex Darien for the Crown. They summoned Dampier and Wafer in June 1697. They paid Wafer to delay publishing his manuscript, wanting its information for themselves. Paterson paid him for the same reason.

The ships sailed from Leith on 14 July 1698, crewed with twelve hundred volunteers. Their intended route was up the east coast of Scotland, round the Orkney Islands to the Atlantic Ocean, down to Madeira, across to the Indies, then into the Caribbean Sea and the Gulf of Darien. Short rations and death were the voyage's themes. The ships were supposed to be victualled for nine months, but the salt beef and pork went mouldy within days, there were weevils in the bread and insufficient oil and butter.

In thick fog, near Aberdeen, the ships lost sight of each other. At Madeira the men swarmed ashore desperate for fresh food. They ate unripe fruit and became ill. They were mistaken for Algerian pirates and attacked. Officers sold their scarlet coats and plumed hats to buy meat.

As they sailed the Atlantic to Antigua, Guadeloupe, and to 'Crab Island' near Puerto Rico, men died like flies: Alexander Alder, Robert Hardy, Andrew Baird, Thomas Fullarton, Peter Wilmot... They died of hunger and disease. A surgeon's mate, Walter Johnson, took too much laudanum for his fever and 'slept till death'. Officers were merciless. With negligible stores, they regretted it if in a day no more than four or five men died. The sick were denied oatmeal or water and left on deck, exposed to bad weather. Those who stole food ran the gauntlet of surviving men, who lashed them with knotted ropes.

It took four months to reach Darien. The *Unicorn*, as it entered the bay, struck sunken rocks. It tore its sheathing and from then on leaked. 'Tis a very wet country' Wafer had written with understatement. 'You shall Hear for a great way together the croaking of frogs and toads, the humming of mosquitoes or gnats and the hissing or shrieking of snakes.'†

The men were exposed to drenching rains, the air was humid, there were violent gales and tornadoes. Here in this mangrove swamp those who had survived the seas were supposed to build New Edinburgh and Fort St Andrew. But scrimp rations and disease had left them weak. 'Our bodies pined away and grew so macerated with such hard work that we were like so many skeletons.'

The settlers lost all interest in their home from home, their squalid New Caledonia where they had come to die. After two months they managed to build rudimentary huts and dig graves for two hundred dead. They ate lizards and pelicans and food scrounged from the Cuna Indians who were hostile to them. They were desperate to leave but had nowhere to go. Ten men who stole weapons from the *Unicorn* and deserted, were caught and put in irons. A plot to sail on a buccaneering cruise in the *St Andrew* was also foiled. There was an epidemic of tropical fever, its symptoms spots, sore eyes and joints, and vomiting bile.

Then the Spaniards, who had garrisons, forts and infantry-men at Carthagena, Santa Maria and Panama, attacked. They sent eight hundred infantrymen to destroy what there was of Fort St Andrew and to burn the huts of New Edinburgh. A northerly wind made it hard for the Scots to flee.

It was near impossible to send letters home for help. When two relief ships the *Olive Branch* and *Hopeful Binning* reached Darien in August 1699 they found ruins and graves. Only one ship, the *Caledonia*, returned to Scotland of the five that had left the Firth of Forth fifteen months previously. It carried no more than three hundred men, many of whom died before it reached the river Clyde.

1701 *A Combate of Neiffells*

THOSE WHO survived such rigours were strong and lucky. Selkirk's behaviour, 'undecent' at fifteen, was violent by the time he was twenty-one. The predicted fortune had not ap-peared, nor the hardship of ye seas reconciled him to family life in Nether Largo. Back home in November 1701 a 'tumult' in his father's house provoked complaints by neighbours. Selkirk, his father, mother, brother Andrew, eldest brother John and John's wife Margaret Bell, were summoned to a disciplinary session of the Church Elders. Largo parish records give detail of the tumult:[†] Andrew took a can of sea water into the house. Selkirk unwittingly drank from it then spat the salt water out. Andrew laughed at him. Selkirk perceived this as an insult, beat him with a cudgel, swore at him, threatened to kill him and tried to go upstairs to get their father's pistol. To block his way, their father sat on the floor with his back to the door. Selkirk hit him. Andrew ran for help to John and Margaret who lived nearby.

Their mother, expecting an all-out fight, left the house. John tried to get their father up off the floor and to the fireside. Selkirk 'caste off his Coate' and challenged John to a 'combate of Neiffells'.[*] Their father intervened to separate them. Selkirk got them both into a neck lock and twisted them to the ground. Margaret tried to drag him off. John ran out of doors. She followed calling back at Selkirk, 'You Fals Loun, will you murder your Father and my Husband both?' Selkirk attacked her too. She was not sure how he beat her, but 'ever since she hath a sore pain in her head'.

He was summoned to appear before the church elders on 25 November. Instead, he went to the nearby town of Cupar. Two days later he was again ordered to attend church, stand in the pulpit and 'be rebuked in face of the Congregation for his scandalous Carriage'. This he did. He confessed he had

*This is apparently bare-knuckled boxing.

sinned by attacking his brothers, 'promised amendment in the strength of the Lord and so was dismissed'.

Such was Selkirk's temper, and violence and retribution in Nether Largo. He wanted again to be at sea with its wider dangers and rewards. He was twenty-three, a navigator, fighter and survivor. Largo held nothing for him. It was intolerable to be laughed at and made to seem foolish by his weakling brother, and to be judged and found wanting by small-town churchgoers who knew nothing of the force of the ocean, the curse of scurvy or the heat of the sun in a Southern sky.

1703 *Fair Speed*

THE *St George* and the *Cinque Ports* left Kinsale on 11 September 1703. That night Dampier, drunk, had 'high words' in his cabin with his First Lieutenant, Samuel Huxford. He summoned the Master, James Hill, and ordered him to turn the ship round, go back to Kinsale and put Huxford ashore. Hill refused to obey this command.

It was not a propitious start or one to inspire confidence in the crew. Dampier took no notice of the Articles of Agreement he had helped formulate and had readily signed. 'Disagreements and Mismanagements defeated our most promising Hopes' the Mate of the *St George*, William Funnell, wrote.[†]

They headed south toward the island of Madeira off the coast of north Africa. Selkirk, as Master, navigated. Dampier praised him as 'the best man on the *Cinque Ports*'. Captain Pickering, 'a main Pillar of the Voyage', was impressed with his skills. On the wide Ocean, in this wooden vessel with canvas sails, Selkirk struggled with time and gravity, the force of winds, the movement of the planets and the turning tides.

Lookout was constant. From the moment he saw Kinsale recede he logged the ship's course and speed by 'dead reckoning', hour by hour, watch by watch, day by day. He referred to uncertain nautical charts and to almanacs of tide tables and the waxing and waning moon.[†] He used a lead plumb line to measure the depth of the sea, a wooden quadrant to measure altitude, a cross-staff to find latitude (the distance north or south of the equator) by the Pole Star, a back-staff to find latitude by the Sun at noon, an azimuth compass to read the magnetic bearings of stars, a steering compass, a nocturnal to gauge the time by night, a sundial to gauge it by day.[†]

He logged the course steered by the compass, the speed of the ship through the water, the magnetic variation of the stars, the drift of the ship away from the wind, the state of the currents and tides, the vagaries of the weather. Errors were cumulative and hunches frequently wrong.

Fifty miles was fair speed in a day. At noon if the sky was clear he checked his dead reckoning latitude against meridian altitude – the angular distance between the horizon and the Sun. But he could not measure longitude – his distance east or west on the earth's surface. The theory of longitude had been understood since classical times. Selkirk knew that relative time and place were determined by the orbiting of the earth on its axis: one revolution of three hundred and sixty degrees in a day, fifteen degrees in an hour. To measure the difference of longitude between the meridian where he was, and some fixed meridian, like perhaps Greenwich, he needed to know *at the same moment* his own local time and local time on the prime meridian. The difference between these, one hour or fifteen degrees, was the difference of longitude. No timepiece had been invented to gauge it. Such a timepiece would have to be accurate for months on end, in a bucketing ship, in every climate.

In 1703 this was a distant dream. The watchmaker who was to 'Find the Longitude' and devise such a timepiece, John Harrison, was a ten-year-old boy.[†] Selkirk, and navigators of his day, tried to find it by calculating the movement of the moon in relation to the sun and the brightest stars. 'Diligent searchers of the heavens' compiled tables of lunar distances. But they did not know what laws controlled the movement of the moon, nor the relative positions of the stars, as time markers, one with another.

Reading the Longitude was a frustrating puzzle and navigation was as much luck as science. It was easy to get grandly lost, to be all at sea, a prey to hostile ships, storms, dwindling rations and the ravages of disease. With the technology of wood, glass and string, with crude magnets, wits and vigilance, Selkirk and his ship tried to be in rhythm with the cool grace of the turning world. There was much to divert him and the crew from such pure pursuit: quarrels, drunkenness, mutiny, weevils in the biscuits and no lemons or limes.

1703 *A Parcel of Heathens*

THE PRIVATEERS reached the island of Madeira after fourteen days. It was of interest to them only for its liquor. William Funnell described it as a pleasant place, but inhabited by Portuguese. A stone wall, cannons and a castle defended its coast. Vineyards covered its southern slopes. Dampier sent boats ashore to load up with casks of wine.

The men sailed on to the Cape Verde Islands. As they anchored at St Jago,* local people clamoured to barter hogs, hens, watermelons, bananas and coconuts, for shirts, breeches and bales of linen. Funnell described them as Murderers, Thieves and Villains: 'They will take your Hat off your Head at Noon-day although you be in the midst of Company and if you let them have *your* Goods, before you have *theirs*, you will be sure to lose them.'†

The privateers considered themselves English, civilised and entitled. They casked fresh water, cut timber for fuel, captured a monkey as a talisman and took Negro men and women as slaves. They gave them meagre food rations and hard lessons in obedience.

They stayed at St Jago for five fraught days. The rows between Dampier and Samuel Huxford became violent. According to Funnell, at midnight on 12 October, Dampier put ashore Huxford with his servant, chest and clothes, then sailed off at four in the morning. Dampier denied this, but others embellished the story. John Welbe, Midshipman on the *St George*, said Dampier pushed Huxford into a boat, threw his sea chest and clothes after him and ordered a Portuguese officer on St Jago, 'a sort of *corregidor*', to lock him up. Huxford managed to get back to the ship, but Dampier ordered him off.

Mr Huxford begg'd of him not to be so barbarous as to turn him Ashore amongst a Parcel of Banditties and Negro's; but desired him to let him lye in the Long-boat; or he would be contented to go before the Mast, rather than go ashore amongst a Parcel of Heathens.†

*Now named Sao Tiago.

Dampier despised this pleading. He connived with Thomas Stradling to pretend to Huxford that he would be allowed to sail in the *Cinque Ports*. Huxford, suspicious, refused to leave the *St George*. Dampier 'with his own Hands took hold of him and thrust him out of the Ship into Lieut. Stradling's Boat'. Stradling bundled him on board a Portuguese merchant ship and the *St George* and *Cinque Ports* sailed off without him.

Huxford was then marooned on St Jago where he died three months later, 'partly with Hunger'. Welbe said he would not have blamed Dampier had he put Huxford ashore in Ireland, but to leave him to die in St Jago was a 'monstrous Barbarity'. He was, he said, unsurprised by his Captain, 'knowing the like Scene of Cruelty was acted by him, when Commander of the *Roebuck*'. Then, too, Dampier had marooned his First Lieutenant, the officer with whom he should have worked in closest accord.

1703 *The Scourge of the Sea*

THE SHIPS cruised south down the coast of Brazil 'not fully resolved what Place to touch at next'. Provisions were low. The men craved fresh meat and vegetables and were sullen when 'great heaps of Stuff not unlike Men's Guts appeared at the bottom of the Beer Butts'.[†]

They caught whatever food they could. On 22 October in deep Atlantic waters they caught a shark, a dolphin and two unfamiliar creatures, a 'Jelly-fish', gelatinous, slimy and green with 'a Monstrous high fin and a long extended mouth', and a large fish they called an 'Old-wife', deep blue with yellow-tipped fins and covered in spots and crosses.

These creatures were drawn, dissected, had bits of their anatomy put aside for medicinal use (sharks' brains were thought good for gallstones) and were boiled for questionable dinner in a large copper cauldron on a brick hearth.

Shark and jellyfish made a change from salt beef and weevil-infested biscuit. White booby birds 'about the bigness of a Duck' landed on the ships and went into the pot. 'They are so silly that when they are weary of flying, they will, if you hold out your Hand, come and sit upon it.' They tasted 'very Fishy' and unless heavily salted made the men sick.

Disease spread. By mid-November fifteen men had fever. The toll rose in the following days. Phlebotomy was the attempted remedy – seven ounces of blood taken from veins on the forehead, arm or foot, or from under the tongue. It was measured in little three-ounce porringers. If that appeared to fail, a concoction of barley, cloves, liquorice and water was proffered. If any ingredient was unavailable something else was substituted.

The ships' surgeons, John Ballett and James Broady, were vague as to why men became ill and what made them well.[†] If the patient recovered, their treatment was assumed to have effected the cure. Those with the 'bloody flux' were prescribed anise or quinces, grated nutmeg, laudanum, or hot bricks to sit on. A few brass pails were available so that 'poore miserable Men in the weakeness may be eased thereon and not constrained to goe to either the Beake Head or Shrouds to ease themselves, nor be noysome to their Fellowes'.

Scurvy, *Scorbutum*, the 'scourge of the sea', claimed more lives than contagious disease, inanition, gunfire, or shipwreck.

Its causes were thought 'infinite and unsearchable'. Perhaps it was a disease of the spleen, or caused by the ship's biscuit, or contracted from dirty clothes and cabins, the damp sea air, the salty pork, cares and grief, or the heat of the day.

Those who observed it wondered at its horrors: lassitude, dejection, infected gums, filthy breath, loose teeth, weak legs, swollen flesh, aches and pains, skin blotched with blue or red stains, 'some broad and some small like flea biting' and 'such costiveness as neither Suppository, Glister, nor any Laxative can put it right. For 14 Daies together they go not to stoole once'.†

Mariners knew that those with scurvy would, if given a chance, suck lemons even on an empty stomach. They had seen those sick with it eat fruit and greens and quickly find their former health. None the less for decades no prescriptive correlation was made between fruit and vegetables and scurvy. It was thought that fresh meat, wine, sugar and 'other comfortable things' would cure it, or oatmeal, or beer mixed with the yolk of an egg, or perhaps the juice of oranges, lemons or limes, or maybe bran, almonds and rosewater, or green ginger, or sweating in steam if that could be arranged, or strong Vinegar and 'a good bathe in the Blood of Beasts'.

James Lind, the naval surgeon who would determine the prevention and cure of scurvy, was not yet born. It was 1747 when he did a controlled trial of antiscorbutics on board a warship, the *Salisbury*. He took twelve sailors all with similar symptoms of advanced scurvy. For six weeks he fed them the ship's standard diet: morning gruel, dinner of mutton broth, pudding and biscuits, supper of barley, raisins, rice, currants, sago and wine. But in pairs he also gave them different daily supplements: cider; elixir of vitriol; vinegar; seawater; two oranges and a lemon; a concoction of nutmeg, garlic, mustard seed, barley water and gum myrrh. The 'most sudden and visible good effects' were from the men who ate the fruit. Lind published these findings in his *Treatise of the Scurvy* in 1753. His was a scientific approach in a speculative age.

But on the *St George* and *Cinque Ports*, in 1703, Ballett and his assistants raked out excrement 'like hard sheep's treckles' with a spatula from the rectums of men with scurvy. 'Warm the spatula and anoint it with oil.' They cut septic flesh away from the sufferers' gums, so that they might better eat their biscuits and meat.

Enough to Terrifie any Man   1703

ON 2 NOVEMBER the ships crossed the equator. The fit were ritually ducked: hoisted up by a rope from the main yard, dropped into the sea from a height, then picked up by boat. Many 'recovered the colour of their skins, which were grown very black and nasty' Funnell wrote.

For days 'much troubled' by gusting southerly winds, the ships made no headway. The men could not hear each other or keep their foothold. Cold, soaked with spray, afraid of being overwhelmed by waves, they had no choice but to secure the guns and anchors and wait for the wind to drop.

The epidemic of fever spread. Captain Pickering lay in his hammock on the *Cinque Ports*, too ill to move. Command passed to his lieutenant, Thomas Stradling, a gentleman mariner only twenty-one years old. Selkirk disliked his high-handedness and complained that neither he nor Dampier adhered to the Articles of Agreement.

On 24 November they reached Le Grande off the Brazilian coast. They anchored in a bay to the south-west of the island. It led to woodland dense with foliage. It seemed like a jungle 'not inhabited by any other than Jaccals, Lyons, Tygers etc. Which in the Night make a most hideous Noise, enough to terrifie any Man.'[†]

In a makeshift way the men 'wooded, watered and refitted their Ships'. The holds were washed with vinegar and water, the deckhead was smoked and the stench subdued. The armourer improvised a forge, coopers repaired casks, carpenters mended masts. But the ships were in disrepair and beginning to leak. Their wood was infested with worms. They were not sheathed underneath and it was not possible to repair them on a remote South Sea island 'having neither materialls nor conveniency'.

Boats sent to the mainland three miles away stockpiled supplies of rum. Graves were dug for the dead. Captain Pickering 'departed this Life'. More than the cursory heaving overboard, his funeral was a ceremony of prayers, homage, cannon fire and burial by a waterfall. Dampier confirmed Thomas Stradling as Captain of the *Cinque Ports* in his place.

Pickering's death was a serious loss. The men had thought him fair. Dampier quarrelled with his new First Lieutenant, James Barnaby. A late night drinking session ended with Barnaby requesting 'Leave to take his Chest and Cloaths out of the Ship'. He said he would rather live among the Portuguese than continue with this voyage. Dampier told him to take his things and go where he pleased.

Barnaby then tried to go ashore. Dampier restrained him,

tied his hands behind his back and left him slumped on deck all
day. Toward evening one of the crew cut him free

and about ten at Night, Barnaby and eight more of our men put their
Chests and Cloaths in the Pinnace, and desir'd some of the Ship's Company
to go in the Boat with them; which accordingly they did, Cap. Dampier
being in his Cabbin quite drunk.[†]

This was mutiny. Twelve men had left the *St George* and
taken its pinnace. Dampier suspected that they planned to
capture a Portuguese bark near the shore then work as pirates.
To foil them he sent letters to the Governor of Rio de Janeiro,
'to acquaint him with the Knavish Part of their Intent'. The
men were not seen again.

Selkirk described their going as a 'great weakening to
the Ship & Damage to the voiage…' Dampier, he said,
'should not have suffered the said Men to go on Shoar'. After
Pickering's death and this mutiny, Dampier, Morgan and
Stradling became more secretive and self-seeking. They
arranged everything between themselves 'without the knowledge of any of the said Ships Company'.[†]

The more the men were excluded from decision making,
the more mutinous they became. They wanted strategy and a
common purpose. They had been at sea five months: no gold
had come their way, they had taken no prizes and their ships
were in disrepair. The captain was drunk and wild-tempered
and the point of the voyage seemed lost.

Alone with the Ship's Monkey   1704

THE TWO SHIPS headed south toward Cape Horn. Dampier
ruled they should not stop again until they reached The

Island. Each day the men became more desperate for comfort. Their dried meat and grain were infested with ants, cockroaches and rats' droppings.

The belongings of those who died of scurvy or fever were vied for in wrangling auctions: a sea chest, bought in London for five shillings, went for three pounds. Shoes, bought for four shillings and sixpence, went for thirty-one shillings. Half a pound of thread that had cost two shillings was sold for seventeen and sixpence.

As they neared Cape Horn the sky turned black. They reefed and furled their sails and waited for the storm. On the night of 4 January 1704 the wind hit so hard it raised the waves to the height of mountains. Rain poured down 'as through a Sieve'. Sheet lightning hit the sea and lit the breaking waves like fire. The ships went where the storm took them. The sea broke over the decks, smashed rails, masts and yards, soaked the men and loosened the anchors. There were no lantern lights or fires for warmth or food. The sick shivered in wet hammocks in the lower decks. A boy aloft lost his hold and drowned in the night. The men crawled the decks, prayed and expected shipwreck.

Only when a corposant, a ball of light, an electrical discharge, appeared on the shattered masthead would they dare to believe that the storm had passed. When grey dawn came the sea was calm. But the ships had lost sight of each other. Dampier supposed they would reunite at The Island. On the *Cinque Ports* Selkirk calculated that he was west of Cape Horn. He turned the ship north into the Great South Sea and headed up the coast of Chile, toward Juan Fernandez.

But Dampier was lost. For three days he headed north to

the east of the Horn. He realised his mistake only when 'contrary to all expectations' he came to islands east of Tierra del Fuego – the Land of Fire. He much resented Funnell's criticism of his navigation skills, the suggestion that he was less than the supreme pilot of these seas. His men braved the Horn again.

The *Cinque Ports* reached Juan Fernandez on 4 February. Its crew of ninety was reduced to forty-two. They were in tattered clothes and they were hungry and sick. They turned on Stradling and accused him of inept command, unfairness and deceit. Selkirk fuelled dissent. He disliked Stradling's upper-class highhandedness. He said that after Pickering's death Stradling had held no consultation with the men and that Articles of Agreement were ignored.[†]

Stradling lost all command. The *Cinque Ports* anchored a mile from the shore, on the eastern side of the Great Bay, in forty-five fathoms of water.[*] The men took the boats to the shore, their sights set on the clear water streams, the goats in the mountains, the crabs and lobsters that scuttled the rocks. 'For two Days the Ship lay as it were without Men.' Stradling stayed marooned on board, alone with the ship's monkey.

Dampier saw The Island but sailed on past. 'Our Captain thought it not to be the right Island' Funnell wrote with scorn. No two charts gave the same latitude. Dampier thought it was at '33:30 South forty-five Leagues west from the coast of Chili'. Its true latitude is 34° 47'S. [**] After several days, when no other land came into view, the ship turned back. Then,

---

[*] A fathom is about six feet. It is determined by the length of the outstretched arms of an average-sized man, to the tip of his longest finger.
[**] A league is about three miles.

'passing by the great Bay, we saw our Consort Capt. Stradling in the *Cinque-Ports*'. Thus Dampier identified his port of call.

Dampier negotiated with the mutineers from the *Cinque Ports*. The ships, he promised, would be 'wooded, watered, heeled and refitted'. The sick would revive on The Island. As soon as they were all refreshed, they would take a prize. Real work was about to begin. Riches were to hand. He was in command of Stradling. He would see that the men's grievances were heard. There would be regular Council meetings. The Articles of Agreement would be honoured. 'By the endless endeavours of Captain Dampier they were reconciled and returned aboard their own Ship again' Funnell wrote.

1704 *Lyon-baiting*

THE ISLAND seemed a depressing place: 'the melancholy howling of innumerable seals on the beach... rocky precipices, inhospitable woods, dropping with the rain, lofty hills, whose tops were hid by thick and dark clouds, on the one hand, and a tempestuous sea on the other.'†

Harsh though it was, after the torment of the sea it proved a haven. Even the slaves seized at St Jago could wash away humiliation in the streams.

The men lit fires and roasted crawfish in the embers, set up tents for the sick, improvised rough dwellings, and plundered the place. A joint of goat, roasted, flavoured with herbs, and served with what they called 'the cabbage palm' boiled, made, they declared, 'a very good Meal, the cabbage as good as any Garden-Cabbage we had ever tasted'.† The palm trees were tall and each had at its head a single fruit. The men could not climb the sheer trunks, so they felled a tree for every cabbage. They strewed The Island with dying wood.

They found fish 'in such plenty that it is almost incredible – Cavallies, Silver-fish, Groopers, Breams and Craw-fish'. They ate these broiled, roasted, or fried in sea-lion oil. They kept a fire burning day and night. In the mornings hundreds of tiny hummingbirds, the males copper-coloured, the females white and metallic blue, were dead by the embers, lured to the light of the flames.

The ships were hauled from the water and careened. Wood was stored, several tons of water, and a ton of sea-lion oil for cooking and for lamps were casked. Funnell took an academic interest in the slaughter of these creatures. He measured a particularly large dead sea lion. It was twenty-three feet long, fourteen and a half feet round, with a seventeen-inch layer of fat.

The Seals are very much afraid of a Man; and so soon as they see him any thing near, they will make to the Water; for they never go far from it. If they are hard pursued, they will turn about and raise their Body up with the Fore-fins and face you, standing with their Mouth wide open upon their Guard: So that when we wanted to kill one, to make Oil, we used commonly to clap a Pistol just to his Mouth, as it stood open, and fire it down his Throat; but if we had a mind to have some Sport with him, which we called Lyon-baiting; usually six, seven or eight, or more of us, would go with each a half Pike in his Hand, and so prick him to Death; which commonly would be a Sport for two or three Hours before we could conquer him. And often times he would find us work enough. But he being an unweildy Creature; and we assaulting him both behind, before, and all round; we must needs conquer. Yet he often put us to the run; and sometimes he would run himself, but knew not which way, for we commonly got between the Water and him.

Thus English pleasures in distant places. The seals were unacquainted with such torment. They had thought The Island a safe place to swim, catch fish, bask on the rocks and protect their young.

1704 *An Insignificant Attempt*

THIS STAY on The Island lasted four weeks. At noon on 29 February a ship came into view. Dampier gave orders to pursue it: 'we got on board all our People, got up our Yards and Topmasts, clapt our Long-Boats on our Moorings, let slip, and got under sail'.

Here was a prize. In their haste for it, the *Cinque Ports* crew left behind spare anchors, cables and sails, their casked water and sea-lion oil and eight men who were hunting goats in the mountains.

It was a dishevelled and disorganised chase. On the open sea they lost two boats. One filled with water and had to be abandoned. In the other, a man and a dog were left adrift without drinking water or food.

The men closed on the ship at eleven that night. Dampier had thought it to be Spanish, but it was a French merchant ship, with a cargo of cordage, in better condition than either of the English ships. It was well manned, twice the weight of the *St George* and with about thirty guns. At dawn the *Cinque Ports* drew near enough to fire ten cannon. The French responded with greater fire. The *Cinque Ports* sheared off, shortened sail and fell astern the *St George*. It could not then use its guns without damaging the *St George*.

Dampier had given orders to pursue this ship only to

placate his mutinous crew. When it came to the fight, his prime
concern was to save himself:

he stood upon the Quarter-Deck behind a good Barricado, which he had
order'd to be made of Beds, Rugs, Pillows, Blankets, etc. to defend him
from the small shot of the Enemy; where he stood with his Fusee in his
Hand. He neither encouraged his men, nor gave them any proper instruc-
tions as is usually required from a Commander at such Times.[†]

The men were desperate for this prize. They needed
consolation for six months of grim living. They wanted, if
nothing else, to replenish their stores and take a ship in better
repair than their own. They had left home in search of gold
and fortune and all they had found were hunger and squalor.
Many had died, thirty were still sick. They fought, broadside
to broadside, for seven hours. Nine men from the *St George*
were killed, more were injured. The French ship was badly
damaged. Its casualties were high with many dead and thirty-
two men wounded, each having lost a leg, an arm or an eye.

Dampier dismissed this battle as 'an Insignificant Attempt'. He had not, he said, 'come thither to fight ffrench-
men'.[†] He 'called out to make Sail, for Fear the Enemy should
clap us on Board and take us'. According to John Welbe that
was the only command he gave during the whole battle.

Squalling winds separated the ships and put an end to
cannon fire. The men feared the frustration of all their hopes
if this ship went free. It would head for Lima. Its captain
would tell the Spanish authorities about them. Merchant ships,
rich with plunder, would then be diverted from the South
American coast.

When the wind dropped, the men wanted to continue the
fight. Dampier would not have it. They rounded on him 'very

much dissatisfied to suffer ourselves to be so baffled in our first Attempt'. He bragged 'that he knew where to go and could not fail of taking to the value of £500,000 any Day in the year'.[†] He was not believed. This captain, when it came to action, hid behind a mattress and gave no orders. He was cowardly, incompetent and usually drunk.

Dampier reassured them that he had a strategy. Sails, boats and men had been left on The Island. They must first return and collect these. Then they would head toward Lima. In that busy stretch of sea they would seize ships without risk, replenish their stores, add to their fleet, take prisoners for whom they could exact ransom. Then under cover of night they would raid the town of Santa Maria where gold was stockpiled from the nearby mines.

Again the two ships headed back to The Island. As they approached, the wind dropped, the sea was calm, and they were forced to row toward the Great Bay. Anchored there were two large French warships. They fired at the *Cinque Ports*, then gave chase.

It occurred to the men that with officers like Dampier and Stradling, no treasure would come their way. As they headed north for the coast of Peru mutiny stirred. Selkirk, Welbe and Clift complained of all the capricious changes of plan. Despite assurances, no council meetings were held. Dampier, Stradling and Morgan made decisions 'hugger mugger' between themselves.

And now there were no spare sails, cables or anchors, no boats, and scarce water and food. Without boats or cables they could not tow their ships if the wind dropped or sails were torn. They could not go ashore in shallow water, or land without being seen at night. Without water they could not cook their scant rations and without cables and anchors they could not moor.

No Small Presumption   1704

THE DEAD were food for creatures of the sea. The injured turned for help to their surgeons. In a small space below the gun deck John Ballett tied splints to fractured bones, raked out bullets embedded in flesh, stitched gunshot wounds, treated burns with quinces and purslain, cracked dislocations more or less back to place and amputated shattered feet and hands.

Ballett thought it wise to amputate in the mornings but never at full moon. His dismembering saws were kept well-filed, clean and in oiled cloths to protect them from rust. He had an assortment of knives, mallets, chisels and stitching needles, some strong waxed thread, rolls of crude cotton and large bowls filled with ashes to catch blood.

The amputee had to give consent and was told that he might die. 'It is no small presumption to dismember the Image of God.'[†] Two strong men held the patient down. The instruments were kept from his view. Ballett, 'with a steady hand and good speed, cut off Flesh, Sinewes and all to the Bone'. He left flaps of skin. He then sawed through the bone, sewed the flaps, stemmed the bleeding with cotton and propped the stump up high with a pillow under it. There was a vessel for amputated limbs 'till you have opportunity to heave them Overboard'.

Even if only the foot was crushed the surgeons took off most of the leg, 'the Paine is all one, and it is most profitable to the Patient, for a long Stumpe were but troublesome'. There were dismembering nippers for amputating fingers and toes.

1704 *A Private Consideration*

THE PRIVATEERS then lay in wait near Callao, the port that served Lima, capital City of Peru. They furled their sails so as not to be seen. The intention was to attack any vessel going in or out of the harbour.

On 22 March two ships headed in. One was the same French galleon they had fought at such cost but failed to take. The men saw this as an opportunity to complete unfinished business. Stradling proposed that the *St George* chase it while the *Cinque Ports* pursued the other smaller ship. Dampier overruled him.

Upon which one of our Men told him to his Face, he was a Coward, and ask'd him, Whether he came to these Parts of the World to fight, or not? And he reply'd, He did not come to fight; for he knew where to make a Voyage, without fighting.[†]

Prizes such as these, Dampier boasted, were 'inconsiderable gains'. The risks and dangers of such skirmishes were not worth the reward. Only the lack of boats, he said, kept him from putting a fortune into the crew's hands.

Only the lack of boats kept the crew from mutiny. Sea water had tainted their food supplies. They were desperate for fresh water, food, action and gold. Without much to do they feuded, and split into gangs. There were violent quarrels and fights, particularly between seamen and landmen. Ralph Clift blamed these fights on Dampier's 'misgovernment':

it was his Duty & in his power to have hindred such Quarrels & ffightings but he only heard the Complaints on one side & the other & never took any Care to prevent them.†

Next morning, in what at first seemed like effortless compensation, they took a Spanish merchant ship *La Ritta* as it left the harbour. Off-guard and unprepared, it put up no resistance. Its cargo was of snuff, lace, wool, silk, tar, tobacco, turtleshell, beeswax, soap, cinnamon, Jamaican pepper, wood and 'a pretty good Sum of Money'.

This might have been a turning point, a success, a justification for the hardship and boredom of it all. But Dampier let the ship sail on. He off-loaded merchandise worth four thousand pounds, and took two of the forty black slaves on board, but he would not let the men rummage the ship, or keep it as a prize. He told the crew that too much plunder would 'be a hindrance to his greater Designs' and that he had no officer good enough to command such a large ship.

No one believed him. Resentment grew. Selkirk claimed he took a bribe from the Spanish commander to let the ship go free: 'a private consideration to Dampier and Morgan for ransom'.

'We were forced to be as well content as we could' Funnell wrote in his journal. Then at dawn next day 'not firing above three guns' the men surprised and took another ship, the *Santa Maria*. It had a cargo of indigo and cochineal and according to Selkirk 'Divers Chests of Silver to the value of £20,000'. Again Dampier would not allow the men to rummage or keep the ship. He took its boats – two launches and a bark – and again in return for a bribe released it. Morgan stowed the captain's silver dinner service, worth £200, in his cabin.

Dampier, when criticised, threatened to blow out the complainant's brains, or maroon him, or throw him overboard. He made airy promises of the gold they would get when they ransacked the town of Santa Maria, of increased dividends and shares for all. He was not believed. There was no trust left among these thieves.

They planned to invade Santa Maria at night by boat. It was across the bay from Panama. To prepare for this, they anchored at Gallo, an island that offered water, wood and a sandy beach. They fitted out the Spanish boats with *pedreros* – small guns that fired stones, nails, broken iron and shot.

For sport they shot large lizards and monkeys. And again they took an easy, unexpected prize – a Spanish bark, commanded by an unwitting Indian. He mistook them for Spaniards and approached them hoping to buy provisions. It was a costly mistake. He and his crew 'lost both themselves, their Vessel and their Money'. On board was a man from Guernsey, taken prisoner by Spaniards while working as a logwood cutter in Campeachy Bay. He had spent two years in a Mexican gaol. He went through a masquerade of conversion to Catholicism to obtain his freedom. A condition of his release was that he stay in Mexico or sail only with Spanish coastal ships.

The privateers sank the bark and marooned its crew. They kept the Indian captain as their pilot. The man from Guernsey was overjoyed to meet his liberators.

A Most Uncomfortable Night

BEFORE THE RAID on Santa Maria, Dampier summoned his officers to a rare Council of War. 'Now it is usual in a Council of War for the youngest Officer to give his Opinion first' Midshipman John Welbe wrote:

But Capt Dampier would always give his own Opinion first: and then, if any of the Officers gave their Opinion contrary to his, he wld fly out in a Passion, and say, If you know better than I do, take you Charge of the Ship. He was always a Man so much self-conceited, that he would never hear any Reason.[†]

On 25 April the *St George* and *Cinque Ports* lay anchored at Point Garachina, near Panama. The Indian pilot was to guide Dampier, Stradling, Funnell, Selkirk and a hundred armed men up river to Santa Maria in the three captured Spanish boats. The rest of the men were to wait vigilantly in the two ships until the boats were back.

A strong ebb tide and a drenching storm hindered the journey up river. The men huddled in the open boats in the dark, 'with much Thunder and Lightning'. They got very wet and 'passed a most uncomfortable Night'. Dampier had a supply of brandy. Stradling asked him to share it with the men. 'Capt Dampier answered: If we take the Town, they will get Brandy enough; but if we don't take the Town, I shall want it my self.'

In the morning five Indians in a canoe paddled by. They were curious as to why a large number of rain-soaked foreigners were lurking in the reed banks. Prompted by Dampier, the captured pilot told them they were from Panama and invited them on board. The Indians paddled off fast. The privateers then shot at them – according to Funnell on Dampier's instruction. Dampier sent a launch after them, but they got away.

It was a serious bungle. The Indians were sure to report to the Spanish authorities that marauding Englishmen were firing nails and stones at innocent passers-by. Ambushes would be laid in Santa Maria and all valuables taken into the hills.

Dampier decided on immediate attack. He ordered Stradling to take the two launches and forty-four men up river to a small village called Schuchaderoes, near Santa Maria. He and the others would follow in the bark when the tide turned. From there they would storm Santa Maria under cover of night.

Stradling and his men could not find the village. Dampier's charts located it on the north bank of the river. They ambushed three Indians in a canoe and forced them to be their guides. Stradling sent five armed men and two of the Indians in the canoe to search out the village. It got dark. The guides became unhelpful. Dogs barked on the south side of the river so the men headed there. As they neared the bank the Indians jumped free. Stradling's men shot into the night but had no idea who or what they hit. Retaliatory blasts of gunfire came from the shore. In the morning when all was quiet the men landed. They found empty huts, fruit trees, chickens, maize and yams. The villagers had fled to the hills.

Next day Stradling went back down river to look for Dampier who had not shown up. He found him by chance. Dampier had missed the mouth of the river and spent a night and a day up a creek. In the captured canoe was a packet of letters. One letter to the Governor of Santa Maria, from the President of Panama, warned him to watch out for 250 armed

Englishmen intent on ransacking Santa Maria. Seven days previously, the President wrote, he had sent four hundred soldiers to reinforce the army there. He was sure by the time the Governor received this letter the additional soldiers would be with him.

Dispirited but not deterred, Dampier, Stradling and eighty-seven armed men, headed for the town in the captured launches and canoe. John Clipperton, William Funnell and thirteen others were to guard the bark until they returned.

They did not have to guard the bark for long. The raiders were back by midnight in disarray and in accusing mood. Several were wounded, one had been killed. A quarter of a mile outside Santa Maria Spanish soldiers had fired at them in three separate ambushes. The men claimed they had scared off these attackers and were ready to invade the town but Dampier ordered a halt. He said there was no point because the Spaniards would have taken their wives, children and all that was valuable out of the town; 'which is always the first thing they do when they hear of an Enemy.'[†]

The men went back to their ships. They had had enough. They despised this captain who planned dangerous manoeuvres then changed his mind at the first whiff of battle. By 6 May all they had left to eat were boiled plantain leaves. The ration was five leaves a day for every six men.

They Departed and Fell Out   1704

AND THEN in a capricious way their luck again appeared to change. At midnight that same day they captured a merchant ship, the *Assumsion*. Its crew, surprised in the dark, put up no resistance. It was loaded with flour, sugar, brandy, wine, tons of quince marmalade, salt, bales of linen and wool. Selkirk said there were enough provisions for four years.

This might have been a high point, a new direction. Passengers on the ship told of eighty thousand Spanish dollars hidden in it at Lima. Selkirk and Funnell were appointed its commanders. The bark used in the abortive Santa Maria raid was sunk, and the *Cinque Ports* and *St George*, with what seemed a great prize, headed for Tobago Island.

Selkirk thought the intention was to anchor at Tobago then 'rummage the ship'. But yet again Dampier and Morgan had their own agenda. They stashed pearls, silk and 'great Ingotts or wedges of silver and also of gold' in the cabin of the *St George*. Then, after four days, without any consultation, Dampier gave orders to set the ship free.[†]

This was the breaking point of the voyage. The men voiced moral outrage. Thieves they might be, but they expected strategy, a sense of fair play, consistency of purpose. Ralph Clift wrote:

After Dampier and Morgan had taken out what they Pleased they would not suffer the Men to rummage the sd Ships but turned them loose again with their Companys and what goods were left in them & would scarsly permit the Men of the sd ships St George & Cinque Ports Gally to take Cloaths tho' they were in great want of them.

Stradling, too, felt cheated. There were no great ingots and wedges for him. He rounded on Dampier called him a drunk who marooned his officers, stole treasure, hid behind blankets and beds when it came to a fight, took bribes, boasted of impossible prizes and when there was plunder to hand let it go. He said he would not continue in consort with him. He would sooner sail alone in the *Cinque Ports*, small though that ship was.

Separated, neither ship had protection against the brutal Spanish *guarda-costa* or other perils of the sea. To part in such a manner was in direct contravention to the Articles of Agreement with the owners. The crew were told to choose their preferred ship and captain. They were not spoiled for choice. Selkirk elected to go with Stradling. All he personally had gained from this last prize was food: flour, sugar and oranges. He too blamed Dampier for the failure of it all:

Capt Dampier refused to give the Ships Companys leave to rummage the Ship, which if he would have done if any Treasure was on board it might have been discovered. And upon his refusing to let the Ships Companys rummage the Ship they departed and fell out each steering their own Course.

Stradling insisted on his crew's share of all booty. Dampier gave him eleven hundred pounds but none of the silver and gold. Stradling gave shares to the men who sailed with him. Selkirk received seventeen Spanish dollars.

On 19 May 1704 Dampier headed back to Acapulco in quest of the Manila treasure ship. Stradling went south down the coasts of Peru and Chile. The *Cinque Ports*, small and ill-equipped and with a crew of only forty men, could not manage without the protection of the *St George*.

Disputes and disagreements flared as rations and hope diminished. Stradling fell out with Selkirk, confined him to the storeroom as a punishment, and gave tasks which should have been his to a junior officer, William Roberts. Alone, in three months the men took only one prize, the *Manta de Cristo*. It was at anchor. Roberts and the gunner, John Knowles, were sent ashore to demand ransom for it. They were captured by the Spaniards and their ransom demand refused. As a reprisal Stradling burned the prize which Selkirk said was anyway of no value.

The ship went on its way, the going was tedious, the weather hot and supplies low. Then it began to leak. It limped near the shore with two men pumping out water day and night. Hope went. It seemed impossible either to return home or to continue with this journey to nowhere. A year into it there was no food, no treasure, a sense of failure and chaos and many dead. Stradling headed for The Island. He hoped to retrieve the masts, sails, stores and men abandoned six months previously and to patch the timbers of this leaking vessel.

1704 *The Worms there doe Eat Shipps*

THE *Cinque Ports* was rowed and towed into the Great Bay of The Island in September 1704. Two of the marooned men guided its boats to the shore. They told of how the French rounded the sheer coast wall of the eastern mountains and took them by surprise. They supposed they had interrogated the man adrift with the dog. The two had escaped capture by hiding in the dense cover of the mountain forest. For days they ate nothing but roots and leaves. They watched the bay and waited until the coast was clear. Their six friends, flushed out by dogs, had surrendered or been shot. The French had taken all the *Cinque Ports*' spare equipment, its anchors, cables, boats.

The Island had been kind to the abandoned men, its winter cool and mild. They had built a hearth of large stones near the shore, and a hut of sandalwood, thatched with grasses. They had cooked seal and goat meat, greens and fish.

Work started to careen and refit the *Cinque Ports*. But it was hard to make progress without replacement masts and rigging. And worms (*Teredo navalis*) had infested the bottom of the ship and devoured its oak timbers.* Selkirk described these timbers as like honeycomb. It was a 'great fault' of Dampier's, he said, not to have had them sheathed at the start with tarred felt and planks. Dampier had claimed 'that there was no manner of Danger from the worms whither they were going'. Yet he had been on similar voyages. In his journal he had described the worms of the Caribbean as 'the biggest I ever did see'. It was foolish to suppose that those of the South Sea might be less gluttonous.†

So there was little point to the efforts of the coopers, smiths, caulkers and sailmakers. Masts were spliced and sails patched but the worm-eaten timbers remained. And the relationship between Selkirk as ship's Master and Stradling the captain became hostile. Selkirk judged that there was no point in continuing their voyage in this leaking ship. It offered no defence against rough seas. They would not be able to attack an enemy ship or take a prize. He told Stradling they should sail no further unless the worms could be killed by breaming and the ship's timbers replaced.

Stradling did not want to linger. The Island was not the place of repose of a year before. He had had enough of its waterfalls, valleys and tumbling streams. He was in need of

---

*Shipworms have two small shells, each about a third of an inch long, with toothed ridges, with which they tunnel into wood. The worm's body is supported by the tunnel as it bores and feeds.

action and fortune, to redeem this voyage and his reputation. He said they would sail again to Peru and try with Dampier for the Manila galleon. At the least they would seize a merchant ship in fair condition that would get them to the East Indies, then home.

Water and oil were casked, wood taken on board, goats tethered, fish salted and turnips and herbs stored. The men were rested, the sick cured or dead. At the beginning of October Stradling gave orders to sail. Selkirk advised the crew to refuse. It was his view that in this ship none of them would go anywhere but to the ocean floor.

Stradling, the gentleman mariner, mocked his caution and belligerence. Selkirk responded with his fists and rage. Stradling accused him of inciting mutiny. He told him he would have his wish and stay on The Island: it was better than he deserved.

Selkirk's concern about the ship was justified. But no one elected to stay with him. No friend. Nor did the others attempt to overrule Stradling's decision. They had lingered enough. Though the ship leaked it was their one chance of achieving a residual dream.

Stradling ordered Selkirk's sea chest, clothes and bedding to be put ashore. Selkirk watched from the beach as the men prepared to leave. He had not wanted the dispute to take this turn. With his brothers and the Largo elders a rebuke in the pulpit, a promise of amendment had settled the score.

He asked Stradling to forgive him, to let him rejoin the ship. He said he would comply. Stradling told him to go to hell, he could be food for vultures for all he cared. He hoped his fate would be a lesson to the other men.

Selkirk watched as the small boats prepared to leave the shore. He lumbered over the stones and tried to get on board but was pushed back. He waded into the water, pleading. He watched as the anchor was drawn and the ship towed to the open sea. The sound of the oars dipping into the water, the calling of orders, the little silhouettes of men as they made fast the cables and unfurled the sails, all imprinted on his mind. There was a light breeze from the west. The ship slipped behind the cliff face and from his view. Against this abandonment the rest of his life had the comfort of a dream.

3

THE ARRIVAL

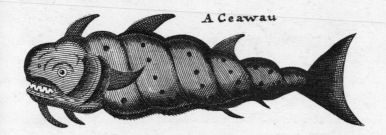

A Ceawau

Monsters of the Deep   1704

ALL COURAGE left him when the ship was gone. The sea stretched out. The line of its horizon was, he knew, only the limit of his sight. The sea that had beckoned freedom and fortune now locked him in.

Thomas Jones, James Ryder, William Shribes, John Cobham... He thought they would come back for him. He stayed by the shore, scanning the ocean. Whatever their fate he now wanted to be with them. If their ship sank he would choose to go down with it. It was his ship too.

Laurence Wellbroke, Martin Cooke, Christian Fletcher, Peter Haywood... they defined his world. The voyage they had made together was for more than gold: it was to show courage, to have a common purpose, to be men. Without them The Island was a prison and he a mariner without a ship, a man without a voice.

The day grew cool, the wind ruffled the water and for a moment a rogue wave or a cloud looked like a sail. His hope was that someone would persuade Stradling to think again. They would come back for him. He would welcome them with fires and food.

He waited outside of time, like a dog. Prayer, he had been taught, had a controlling force. He invoked God, to sort this mess out. He prayed in a cajoling way. He felt rage at Stradling. Even Dampier, mad and drunk, marooned Huxford in the company of men. But Stradling had marooned him, Selkirk, with calculated malice and mocked him as the boat rowed off.

He did not leave the shore. He clambered over the stones to the western edge of the bay, wanting the wider view of the ocean. The fur seals bottled and dived, surf broke over the rocks. He was trapped in the bay by sheer cliffs. He clambered back to the eastern edge by the fast-flowing stream where trees grew close to the water's edge.

The sun dipped down, the air cooled, the mountains loured. Dark came and the moon cut a path across the ocean. All night the seals howled. These were monsters of the deep. He feared they would encroach and break his limbs with their jaws. He fired a bullet into the air. For a minute the bay seemed quiet. Then it started again, a croak, a howl. This Island was a place of terror.

In his argument with Stradling, he had seen The Island as a place of plenty and comfort. The safe bet. He had reasoned that survival would be possible, even pleasurable. That rescue would soon come. But there was fear in the dancing shadows of night. There was malice focused on him. A hostile presence sensed his every move. He feared cannibalism. That he would be taunted and devoured.

The wind surged through the valley, the wind, he was to learn, that was strongest when the moon was full. It uprooted trees. They swished and crashed. The sound merged with the breaking waves, the calling seals and the cries of creatures preyed on at night.

Griping of the Guts 1704

IT WAS early spring and around him life regenerated, but he hated The Island, its inaccessible terrain, ferocious waterfalls and gusting winds. A faint breeze at night would stir to whirlwind. It was as if the wind was born in these mountains.

Time passed. 'He grew dejected, languid, scarce able to act.' He stayed by the shore, drank rum, chewed tobacco, and watched the sea. He stared so hard and long he only half remembered he was searching for a sail. Often he was deceived by the blowing of a whale or the refraction of light.†

There was a makeshift hut by the shore, of sailcloth, sandalwood and rushes. He put his possessions in it and envied those who had built it. They had got away.

He had with him his clothes and bedding, a pistol, gunpowder, bullets, a hatchet, a knife, a pot in which to boil food, a bible, a book of prayers, his navigation instruments, and charts on how to read the imprisoning sea. He had two pounds of tobacco, and a single flask of rum. He had bits of food, enough for three meals – quince marmalade and cheese – but no bread or salt. He suffered when his liquor flask was empty. Liquor brought oblivion.

'At first he never eat any thing till Hunger constrain'd him, partly for grief and partly for want of Bread and Salt; nor did he go to bed till he could watch no longer.' He drank from the streams when thirsty, splashed himself with water if he itched, or stank or was hot. He pissed where he stood, shat on the stones, ate turnips and watercress pulled from the earth, picked up turtles and lobsters that crawled the shore and scooped out their flesh with his knife.

He became thin and weak. He wanted death and to be gone from this fate. It calmed him to suppose that if no ship came his gun to his temple would end his life. He thought of drowning, of swimming toward the horizon until exhausted. But he had seen sharks devour the corpses of men buried at sea. He had seen a shark tear the leg from a boy who fell from the masthead.

And then it seemed The Island would kill him, would do the deed. The turtle flesh 'occasion'd a Looseness' that twisted his guts like knives, his shit was liquid, he retched and vomited and supposed he would die. He crawled into his bedding and forgot to hope for the ship's return.

The pain abated, he survived. Survival was all. He collected twigs and branches of sandalwood, started a fire with the flint of his gun, boiled water in his kettle and infused it with mint that grew in the valley and with Malagita pepper which he thought to be good for Griping of the Guts.

1704-9 *Alone Upon This Island*

SELKIRK SUPPOSED in time a ship would come, fatigued by the sea, needing a harbour, but time for him might stop. He had seen bleached human skulls on deserted islands, abiding proof of the marooned.

Other men had survived The Island: the two who escaped the French. In six months they suffered no extravagant hardship though they did not linger when dubious rescue came. And Will, the Miskito Indian – it was twenty years since his rescue. The remains of his hut and hearth were high in the mountains, engulfed by ferns. Like Will, Selkirk could forge harpoons and lances from the metal of his gun, strike fire from sticks, survive on seal and cabbages and fashion clothes from animal skins.

And Dampier had told of a shipwreck, before Will was abandoned, in the Great Bay where only one man reached the shore alive. 'He lived alone upon this Island five years before any Ship came this way to carry him off.'

Marooned men fended until rescue came: Pedro de Serrano, stranded on a barren Pacific island, drank the blood of turtles and survived seven years without fresh water, though he went insane. Philip Ashton, captured by pirates in 1700, then abandoned on Roatan Island in the Bay of Honduras, was attacked by snakes and a wild boar, but did not die. In the manner of counting blessings Selkirk might deem himself fortunate. There were worse scenarios than his own. He was as strong as any man. He could endure The Island for months or even years.

He thought of escape, of a raft with branches bound with the entrails of seals, of a hollowed canoe. But the nearest land was Valparaiso, six hundred miles north. Were he by fluke to survive the treachery of this ocean, its capricious currents, the violence of its waves, the appetite of sharks and the heat of the sun, if the *guarda-costa* caught him they would show no mercy. They made it a rule never to allow an Englishman with knowledge of these seas ever to go free. Were he to reach the mainland he would be consigned to the workhouse or the mines, put in leg irons, tortured for information about his fellow privateers. At best, murdered.

If a French ship came to The Island he would surrender and hope for mercy, but never to the Spanish. He would make a lair, a hideaway, high in the mountain forest, in case they came.

So he hoped for rescue and feared dying uncomforted in this overwhelming place. He looked out over the ocean thinking Dampier, Clipperton, Funnell, Morgan, Bellhash might return him to the world he knew. Their misfortune was his hope. The *Cinque Ports* might limp back, leaking like a sieve. He supposed there would be further mutinies on both ships. More men would turn on Dampier. He was an adventurer, a seasoned navigator, but he could not manage men. Mutineers would leave him, take prize ships, fly the bloody flag, the pirates' flag, and try their luck. The two ships might now be six.

Selkirk's Island was the best to careen, to water, to eat fresh food. Here was good anchorage. Whoever came, he would give them greens and goat broth to cure their scurvy. His fire would dry their clothes and warm their bones. They would restore in the mountain air. He would welcome any of the men, except Stradling. He would sooner be marooned for ever than see Stradling again.

And so he became a watchman by occupation. His obsession and abiding fear was that he would miss a ship that passed or be surprised by an enemy. He watched in the first light of the morning, at noon and at dusk. Behind the bay he climbed to his lookout, his vantage point. He scanned the encircling sea. He surveyed The Island, its tormented forms, its peaks and valleys, the islet of Santa Clara, the forests of ferns. Day after day he did not see his ship of rescue. He saw no ship at all.

Here was a paradox of freedom: he was free from responsibility, debt, relationship, the expectations of others, yet he yearned for the constraints of the past, for the squalor and confinement of shipboard life.

Hunger and thirst were diversions. He ate roots, berries, birds' eggs. He shot seals and sea birds. A goat stared at him with curiosity. He killed it with a cudgel, boiled it with turnips, flavoured it with pimento. Rats scuttled in the undergrowth, waiting their share.

The Fragrance of Adjacent Woods   1704-9

DAYS ELIDED into weeks and months. Whatever The Island had, he could use, whatever it lacked, he must do without.

He pined with 'eager Longings for seeing again the Face of Man'. He was alone on a remote piece of land surrounded by ocean. Chile was 400 miles away, Largo 6000. He was an unsociable man, but disagreement and provocation were preferable to this. Had Stradling left him with a Negro slave, they might have built a boat, farmed goats. Had he left him with women prisoners, he would have peopled The Island and been served.

This fate seemed like a curse. His father had warned that his temper would cost him his life, and opposed his going to sea with the privateers. If he returned to Largo he would make amends, work as a tanner, find a wife.

His mother, he supposed, would pray for him. Texts from the Bible. All that happened was God's will. God acted with surprising vengeance, but good intention. The Bible was the word of God. It was the Truth. God created all things, owned and controlled the lot. He made the world in seven days and man in his own image. He was benevolent. He had a purpose, a grand design.

'It was Selkirk's manner to use stated hours and places for exercises of devotion, which he performed aloud, in order to keep up the faculties of speech, and to utter himself with greater energy.'[†] Sometimes as the sun rose lighting the woodland of sandalwood trees and huge ferns (*Blechnum cycadifolium*), their fronds unfurling like wakening snakes, the mountain he called the Anvil rising three thousand feet behind him, cloud trapped on its peaks, he read from the Bible, the only narrative text he had. He read of Sodomie and Beastialitie in Leviticus and of Heaven and Redemption in the Gospels. He mumbled the psalms and appeals of his church: 'Hear O Lord my Prayer, give Ear to my Supplication, hear me in Thy Justice, I stretch forth my Hands to Thee; my Soul is as Earth without Water unto Thee, Hear me speedily O Lord; my Spirit hath fainted away. Turn not away Thy Face from me.'

Such lamentations yielded no change in his circumstances, but had a consoling force. He did not care too much about the sense of what he intoned. It was vocabulary he would not otherwise have used and feared to lose. He hoped that God was half-way human enough to get him out of this hole. Only God and Stradling knew he was marooned.

Withdrawal from tobacco left him light-headed. It had been an addiction for fifteen years. He wondered if there was some substitute opiate on The Island, some other leaf to chew. But he did not experiment. Foxglove and hemlock he knew could kill. Dampier had warned against eating plants that birds rejected.

Activity dispelled depression. He kept busy. And on a day when the sky was clear and the valley still, his mood lifted. He felt vigorous, reconciled. He grilled a fish with black skin in the embers of a fire, ate it with pimentos and watercress and forgot to deplore the lack of salt. Around him humming-birds whirred and probed. Mosses, lichens, fungi and tiny fragile ferns, epiphytes, *Hymenophyllum* and *Serpyllopsis*, covered the trunks of fallen trees.

He resolved to build a dwelling and accrue stores. He chose a glade in the mountains a mile from the bay, reached after a steep climb. Behind it rose high mountains, wooded to the peak. This glade had the shade and fragrance of adjacent woods, a fast, clear stream, lofty overhanging rocks. From it he had watched mist fill the valley and dissipate with the morning sun. White campanulae grew from the rocks, puffins nested by the ferns. A little brown and white bird, the rayadito, swooped for insects. Clumps of parsley and water-cress grew by the stream.

Pestered by Rats   1704-9

THE RANDOM yield of The Island became his tools, weapons, furniture and larder. By the shore he found nails, iron hoops, a rusty anchor, a piece of rope. With fire and stones he forged an axe, knife blades, hooks to snare fish, a punch to set wooden nails. He carved a spade from wood and hardened it in glowing embers. He hollowed bowls and casks from blocks of wood. He turned boulders and stones into larders for meat, a pestle and mortar, a hearth and a wall.

He liked goat meat, but often the goats he shot crawled to inaccessible rocks to die. When his bullets and gunpowder were finished he felt undefended, on a par with creatures that scurry for cover at a sudden sound. Without gunfire, he caught goats by chasing them. Out of their horns he carved cutlery.

On either side of the stream he built huts of pimento wood. He thatched their roofs in a lattice of sandalwood. The cruder hut was his larder and kitchen, the larger was his dwelling. On a wide hearth of stones, he kept a fire burning night and day, its embers banked high. His wooden bed was on a raised platform, his sea chest held such possessions as he had. He scraped, cleaned and dried the skins of the goats he killed, in the way he had learnt from his father. With a nail he made eyelets then joined the hides with thongs of skin. He lined the walls of the hut with these skins. The place smelled like a tanner's yard, it smelled like home.

Home shielded him from squalling winds and the threat of night. From his bed he saw the ocean lit by stars, the morning sun above the eastern mountains. The seals were quieter when they finished breeding. Other sounds amplified: the clamour of birds, the waterfalls.

This glade defined where he felt safe, but 'his habitation was extremely pestered with rats, which gnawed his clothes and feet when sleeping'. Their forebears had jumped from

European ships. Pregnant at four weeks, they gave birth after three weeks' gestation, had litters of eighteen, became pregnant again immediately, and lived for two years. They ate bulbs, shoots, carcasses, bones, wood and each other. They left spraints of urine wherever they went and their fur was infested with lice and fleas. Their appetites were voracious and their most active time, the pitch of night. The Island housed them in millions, white, grey, black and brown. As he slept they gnawed his clothes and the bone-hard skin of his feet. He would wake to hissing fights. He slung pebbles at them, but in seconds they resumed.

Equally fecund were the feral cats. They too came from Spanish, French and English ships. He enticed them with goats' meat wanting them to defend him against the rats. Kittens in particular within days were tame. 'They lay upon his bed and upon the floor in great numbers.' They purred to see him, settled in shafts of sunlight, curled round his legs. To them he was a gentle provider, a home maker.

In the face of this feline army the rats kept away. Instead he endured the cats' territorial yowls, their mating calls and acrid smells. He talked to them, they made him feel less alone. 'But these very protectors became a source of great uneasiness to him.'

For the idea haunted his mind and made him at times melancholy, that, after his death, as there would be no one to bury his remains, or to supply the cats with food, his body must be devoured by the very animals which he at present nourished for his convenience.[†]

To ensure his meat supply, he lamed kids by breaking their back legs with a stick. He then fed them oats gathered from the valley. They did not equate their pain and curtailment with him and were tame when he approached them with food.

So he became The Island's man. Monarch of all he surveyed.[†] He swam in the sea, washed in the streams, rubbed charcoal on his stained teeth. His beard that was never cut merged with the tawny hair of his head. His shoes wore out but he did not try to repair them. The soles of his feet became as hard as hooves. He ran barefoot over rocks. 'He could bound from crag to crag and slip down the precipices with confidence.'[†]

The seals and sea lions ceased to be a threat:

merely from being unruffled in himself he killed them with the greatest ease imaginable, for observing that though their Jaws and Tails were so terrible, yet the Animals being mighty slow in working themselves round, he had nothing to do but place himself exactly opposite to their middle, and as close to them as possible, and he despatched them with his Hatchet at will.[†]

Their fat was cooking oil, their fur his bedding, shared with pale fleas and ticks that burrowed and blistered under his skin. He gouged these out with a wooden pin.

As time passed he ceased to imagine threat from monsters or cannibals. Nor was he troubled by the moan of the wind, the calling seals, the chirps and screechings of The Island. His hut, cats and goats created a semblance of home. He adapted to The Island's ways.

1704 *Hard Labour*

HE WAS RIGHT about worms eating the *Cinque Ports*. In his view 'The Mexican Worm was larger, and eats the Bottoms of the Ships more on its Sea-Coasts, than any other place'.[†] After a month the ship sank near Malpelo, a small barren island off

94

the Peruvian coast. Stradling and thirty-one men got to the shore on two rafts. The others drowned.

This island offered none of the abundance of Juan Fernandez. They existed at the brink of life on chance catches of fish and birds and drank the blood of tortoises because there was no water. Eighteen survived, then surrendered to the *guarda-costa* as an alternative to starvation. They were fed, shackled and marched overland via Quito and Cisco to prison in Lima. 'The Spaniards put them in a close Dungeon and used them very barbarously.'|

As prisoners they were left to rot, or used in the gold and silver mines and workhouses. 'Those that are put in Workhouses are chain'd and imploy'd in carding Wool, rasping Logwood etc.' They were in the company of 'Mullattoes and Indians, but no Spaniards, except for the worst of Crimes'.

A sort of freedom could be bought if the bribe was high. 'Turning Papist' was another way. True Englishmen thought this the surrender of their souls and worse than death. Converts were baptised, then employed as servants to men of note, or used as money-making curiosities. One privateer who ostensibly converted, was baptised in the Cathedral of Mexico City, then displayed in markets. The ritual was to sprinkle oil on his tongue and pour oil on his head. The 'small parcels of Cotton' used to rub these off were then sold to Penitents for an ungodly fee, with a claim to their divine properties 'because taken off the Head of a converted Heretic'.

Stradling spent four years in prison in Lima. He escaped twice. The first time he made toward Panama in a stolen canoe. He hoped to cross the Isthmus then get to Jamaica with an English trading sloop. He paddled twelve hundred miles, was recaptured, thrown back into gaol and warned that if he tried it again he would be sent to the mines. He tried it again and was taken prisoner by a French ship bound for Europe. From there he made his way home to Britain, penniless and ill.

1704 *Rogue, Rascal, Son of a Bitch*

NOR DID Dampier's fortunes improve. The worms were at it in the *St George* too. Funnell said its timbers were so badly eaten they were as thin as a sixpence. 'We could thrust our thumbs quite through with ease.'

Yet still Dampier aimed for 'the chiefest end of the expedition', the Manila treasure galleon. In pursuit of it, he voyaged north in 'dirty squally weather, with much Thunder and Lightning, and very uncertain Gales'. The men survived on fish and turtles until they seized a small craft, bound for Panama, with a cargo of flour, sugar and brandy. On it were more letters to the President of Panama. They learned that two Spanish Men-of-War, armed with twenty-four-pound brass guns and five hundred soldiers and seamen, were lying in wait for them near Guayaquil.

On 22 July they fought one of these warships. According to Welbe, at ten in the morning Dampier gave orders to attack. Welbe advised him to wait 'till we had the Advantage of the Sea-Breeze',

and then we might be sure of getting to the Windward of her; but if we tack'd the Ship then, as he intended to do, we sh^{ld} lose the Advantage of the Sea-Breeze, and be sure to go to the Leeward of her. But he w^{ld} not consent to it, but took his own Way, and immediately tack'd the Ship. And as I said,

so it happen'd; for we were not able to fetch to the Windward of her. But if
Capt. Dampier had taken my Advice...†

As ever, Dampier took no one's advice. He blamed his
crew for the botch-up. He called them 'a Parcel of Fellows
who were Perpetually drunk... They were always Doing
something they should not; and did not think me worthy their
Council'. They had, he said, 'sprung my Fore-Top Mast in the
Night, so it immediately came by the Board. By this I was ut-
terly deprived of means to get a windward, or anything else.'

Insults were exchanged. The men told him he was not fit
to captain a ship and that his language was 'very base and
abusive'. He should not call them *Rogue, Rascal, Son of a
Bitch* and other such vulgar Expressions'.

They hoisted 'the bloody Flag', instead of the English
ensign of a commissioned privateer and fought the ship for
themselves. Funnell said they fought from noon to dusk. 'We
went to it as fast as we could load and fire.' They made little
impact and counted themselves fortunate that only two of
their men had their hands and faces blasted. The Spanish ship,
unharmed, sailed away in the dark.

Dampier feared that his Master, Mr Bellhash, and his First
Mate, John Clipperton, were 'on the Watch to overset the
Voyage'. The crew had split into marauding gangs. At the
island of Gallera, twenty armed men went ashore to loot and
scavenge. Islanders fled to the mountains 'with their Wives
and Children and all they had'. The gang ransacked their huts,
stole wood from a half-built bark, and took another bark with
two masts and square sails, loaded with plantains. They
named it the *Dragon*.

The ostensible plan was to fit this out as a consort, the

better to fight the treasure ship. At St Lucas the *St George* was hauled ashore. It was encrusted with barnacles and leaking. The carpenters could do no more than patch leaks with nails and oakum. While they worked, its ammunition and provisions were stored on the *Dragon*. On 2 September twenty-one men, led by Clipperton, demanded money and silver from Dampier, boarded the *Dragon*, and left under cover of night.

In a ship of holes with scarce arms and a reduced crew, the *St George* sailed on toward Acapulco. The men ate guanos and pelicans. They saw the 'Vulcans of Guatimala' spewing flames. On 9 October a small prize yielded provisions. Her captain, Christian Martin, an adventurer brought up in London, knew the South Sea. On a previous disputatious voyage he had marooned himself on the island of Gorgona, then escaped to freedom on a raft of tree trunks with two shirts for a sail and a large bag filled with oysters fixed to the mast.

Martin helped them locate the Manila galleon. It was called the *Rosario* and they sighted it on 6 December near the 'Vulcan of Collima'. It was a well-built ship, armed with twenty-four-pound cannon. The *St George* had only four five-pounders. Martin advised that the one chance of success was to draw alongside by stealth then board with speed.

Dampier vacillated and was as ever drunk. The *Rosario*, supposing the *St George* to be friendly, hoisted the Spanish ensign and fired a greeting shot to its leeward. Welbe and others urged Dampier to fly Spanish colours. Instead, he hoisted the English flag and gave orders to fire.

The *Rosario* 'sprung her luff and got to windward' and prepared to batter the *St George* to pieces. The boatswain on the *St George* urged the helmsman to edge near, so that they could board quickly. Dampier swore he would shoot him through the head if he did so. The *Rosario* cannon hit the *St George* below water, hit the 'Powder Room' and blasted planks out of the stern. Welbe told Dampier the ship was sinking: 'The captain cried out, Where is the canoe? Where is the canoe? And was for getting into the boat to save his life, which showed what man of courage and conduct he was.' Dampier said the men were not in a fit state to board anything. They were all 'Drunk and Bewitch'd though Clark, the Mate, who was Potent in Liquor, cry'd Board, board her'.

As the *St George* sheared off, the carpenters again tried to plug holes in its timbers. Welbe said Dampier left no orders with anyone but went to his cabin with a supply of liquor, ordered a sentry to guard the door 'that no Body should disturb him', and did not wake until eight next morning.

The Manila ship sailed toward Lima, its treasure intact. The crew of the *St George* wanted to go home 'knowing we could do no good in these Parts, either for our selves or Owners; having Provision but for three Months and that very short; and our Ship being ready of herself to fall in Pieces'.†

His Agility in Pursuing a Goat   1704-9

SELKIRK VIEWED The Island as his, though he did not paint it, or describe it. A rainbow arched the sea, the night was lit by stars, the morning sun coloured the sky, and all for him alone. The Island had offered itself to him and made him safe. He carved the days of his banishment on a tree in the grove of his home. The past might not have existed, he had so few mementoes of it.

Sandalwood burned light and fragrant. In his lesser hut he stored food: turnips, cabbages and pimentos, dried oats, parsley and purslain and little black plums, gleaned from an orchard high in the mountains. He kept his food in boxes he had made, secured with stones and goatskins. On his improvised table with the knife he had honed, he prepared his meals each day: a broth of goat and cabbage, flavoured with herbs, a roasted fish, baby seal fried with turnips, boiled lobster with oatcakes. He drank water and infusions of herbs, simmered plums for their juice, turned them into a kind of jam.

His shirt and breeches got torn to tatters in the forest foliage, the rasping tree ferns, and giant roots. He tailored himself a skirt and jerkin out of goatskin and sewed these garments with thongs of skin. 'He had no other Needle but a Nail.' Out of the bale of linen in his sea chest he fashioned shirts, 'and stitch'd 'em with the Worsted of his old Stockings, which he pull'd out on purpose'.[†]

He was, he thought, a better cook, tailor and carpenter than before, and a better Christian too.[†] Whatever he did on The Island seemed neither right nor wrong. He killed seals, bludgeoned goats, masturbated against palm trees, picked puffins' eggs from their nests and intoned psalms: 'I am become like a pelican of the wilderness; I am like a night raven in the house. My days have declined like a shadow and I am withered like grass. Hear O Lord, my prayer. Turn not away Thy face from me.'

Apart from such borrowed incantations he had no use for words. He learned The Island the way a child learns language, its moods and reiterations, the meaning of its hills. He tutted at the cats and kids and grunted as he pursued goats. Deceived that he was one of them, they turned to greet him until they smelled his sweat, heard his mumbling and saw the cudgel he wielded.

His exercise and lust of the day was hunting and fucking goats. 'He kept an Account of 500 that he killed while there, and caught as many more which he mark'd on the Ear and let go.' His tally was of their size and agility and the quality of the chase; a chart like those kept of the variations of the tide, the phases of the moon or the days of his captivity on The Island.

Goats worked out at about five a week. Most days he had a go. He devised various ruses for catching them. He would crouch on a concealed rock by their watering hole. As they drank at the stream he would leap on one and cudgel its head. Or he would pursue a herd down the mountain to the shore. In confusion and fear they jostled together and made easy prey. Or he would tie a looped thong with a circle at its centre across the path they took. One would catch its horns or neck in the loop. As it panicked and twisted the thong tightened.*

Fucking goats was perhaps less satisfying than the buggery and prostitution of shipboard life, the black misses of heathen ports. It lacked fraternal exchange. But Selkirk was an abandoned man. On The Island, at the day's end, he would have

---

*It occurred to me, when I read of it in Woodes Rogers' journal, that Selkirk's ear notching had a sexual reference. An Islander, Jaimie Sidirie, told me in 1999 that 'Selkirk cut the goat because he had used it.' It still went on, he said. It was a mark of conquest. 'It's the same story round the world when a man is alone.' Jaimie also told me of his own ways of catching and slaying goats when unarmed.

Chroniclers of Lord Anson's expedition to the South Sea, in 1741, wrote of venerable slit-eared goats on The Island. They supposed this ear-piercing to be Selkirk's work. But he had left The Island thirty-three years previously, and goats live about eighteen years.

liked a woman to cook for him and provide. He might have preferred it had the goats been girls.

His Agility in pursuing a Goat had once like to have cost him his Life; he pursu'd it with so much Eagerness that he catch'd hold of it on the brink of a Precipice, of which he was not aware, the Bushes having hid it from him; so that he fell with the Goat down the said Precipice a great height, and was so stun'd and bruis'd with the Fall, that he narrowly escap'd with his Life, and when he came to his Senses, found the Goat dead under him. He lay senseless for the space of three days and was scarce able to crawl to his Hutt, which was about a mile distant, or to stir abroad again in ten days.[†]

He computed the time that had passed from the waning moon. He supposed he might die on The Island, lie unburied and be food for the cats.

1706 *Thorny Shrubs and Scented Laurels*

IT WAS JULY when he fell. There was a light fall of snow. In the voyages he had made death was all that many booty seekers found. But it was death in the company of men, not alone in an implacable place like this.

The fire went out and he scarcely ate. When he was able to limp from his hut, he thanked God for not taking his life. He gathered a mound of dried grasses as tinder, crouched over it and on his knee rubbed together two pieces of sandalwood. The effort seemed endless, the sticks got warm and worn, his body ached, the cats sat around. A desultory spark hit the tinder and expired. He rubbed on. It had worked for Neanderthal man, it must work for him. He rubbed until it happened. The elemental change. Showers of light, grey smoke then flames.

He vowed never again to let this fire die, to guard it night and day, feed it, bank it. It gave him light and heat, it was a symbol of hope, a focus of rescue, a beacon to the seas that he might be saved.

As the days passed, day after day after day after day, he got inured to solitude. Company was not essential. His relationship was to The Island. He was a rough man but it seduced him. He had so much time to observe the sunlight on the sea, the mist in the valley, the shapes of the mountains, the shadows of evening. He came to know The Island's edible plants, its thorny shrubs, scented laurels and palms, its useful animals and freshwater springs, its natural shelters, birds and fishes, its lizards that basked in the sun, its rocks covered in barnacles. He carved a map of it on a piece of wood.

Things he had thought essential he found he could do without: salt, liquor, tobacco, shoes. He built a walled enclosure, drove a few kids in, their mothers followed, he turned the kids out and started a small herd. He churned their milk to a kind of cheese.[†] He made a raft from the trunks of palm trees, carved a double-ended paddle and keeping close to the shore on a calm day explored the bay between what he called Great Rock and Great Key, around what he called Rough Point and Rocky Point. He came to a cave and thought it a place where a man might shelter. He fished from this raft and from the rocks and kept a few clawing lobsters at the brink of life in a barrel of seawater. In all that he did he thought ahead, in case the weather turned foul, in case he again was ill, in case an enemy came.

He carved a little flute, blew a few notes and imagined his tamed animals listened and moved to his tune. He was afraid of nothing on his island. Only of who or what might come to challenge his hegemony.

1707 *The Stretch of the Mountains, the Fact of the Trees*

SELKIRK SAW the irony of his fate. He had crossed the world in search of fortune and ended up with nothing. Less than when he began. He was marooned and penniless and resembled a goat.

Such treasure as he had was The Island. Such music as he heard was the wind in the mountains, the sea, the noises of creatures who cared for each other and nothing for him. The Island imposed a terrible boredom. He yearned to leave it. It was the death of ambition. It tested him to the edge of endurance. And yet in surviving it he found a strength.

He had times of anger, when the goats eluded him, when the fire smouldered and could not be coaxed to flame; times of satisfaction when turnips sprouted and there was an abundance of plums. He found repose in the glade of his home when he had fished and hunted, stoked the fire, fed the cats, milked the goats, done all that he had to do to stay alive.

But it was not the frustration and rewards of practical things that informed and changed him. Nor was it The Island's scenic views, its turquoise ocean, pink horizon, tints and hues; rather it was the way it defeated everything that visited it, gave it food, provided shelter, dished out death. There were times when the intensity of the place overwhelmed him. Times that had nothing to do with the incantation of prayer, or of fear or danger. It was the sheer stretch of the mountains, the fact of the trees. It was as if The Island claimed him with its secrets, its essential existence, made him a part of its rhythms, turned him fleetingly into more than he was. In his piratical soul he knew that he would die in this place, whether he was rescued from it or not.

The Craters of the Moon 1707

STOOPING TO DRINK Selkirk saw a distorted reflection – a tangle of beard and hair, a weathered skin. He became immune to the bites of insects and to the ferocity of the sun. He tied his hair with a goatskin thong, used his nails as claws. He kept his knife and cudgel strapped to his waist.

He swung from lianas with the grace of an ape, ran faster than any creature on The Island, got the fruits of the cabbage palms by climbing. No creatures preyed on him. No scorpions or tigers. Only once he thought he saw a snake. It startled him in the long grass.

Though he looked like a goat, there were times when he thought like a man. With the mind of a mariner, he thought of the forces and laws of nature by which the world might be understood. He had among his navigational instruments a glass that made the stars seem near. He observed the phases of the moon and how these influenced the tides. He watched the constellations of Orion and Andromeda, the light of the planets – Mercury, Venus, Saturn, Mars. With the hope that he might help to 'find the so-much-desired longitude' he tried to chart the movement of the moon against the stars.

It occurred to him that the stars he saw, like the horizon of the ocean, were also only the limit of his vision. He had learnt from Nicolaus Copernicus that illusion was delusion, that the sun was not moving across the sky. The truth held secrets and paradoxes. It occurred to him that time might move in the opposite direction from what was supposed, that the beginning of the world was in fact its end, that the men on the *Cinque Ports* were probably dead, washed by the ocean to the start of their lives.[†]

1705-6 *We have Iron Crows on Board*

THE CREW of the *St George* reckoned that the escape of the Manila galleon deprived them of two million pounds. As it sailed east, proud in the wind, its masts no more than splintered, its flags flying high, they urged Dampier to head for home. His response was that 'he would not come home with his hands in his pockets'.†

Nor would he come home with his crew. They mutinied. At the end of January 1705, in desperation, he summoned them all to a meeting

and having given them a dram of Rum or Brandy or some other strong Liquor desired all who were willing to go along with him upon their own accounts exclusive of the Owners to go on the quarter-deck.†

It was an invitation to turn pirate and abandon any vestigial obligation to the agreements made. But 'no more than twenty-eight Men and Boys, and most of them Landmen' were willing to go along with him. The others deserted in Christian Martin's ship. The purser Edward Morgan, his partner in crime, went, so did William Funnell, John Welbe and thirty-one men. John Ballett the surgeon was the only officer to stand by him.

Their departure was violent. Dampier said Bellhash, the Master, 'took me by the Throat, and Swore if I spoke a Word they would Dash my Brains out'. They turned all prisoners ashore to prevent him finding the route home. They demanded the keys to the powder room and arms' chest. When he refused to hand these over, Morgan said, '"We have Iron Crows on Board, they are as good Keys as we desire," and with that broke 'em open.' They stripped the ship of arms, food, liquor, silver plate and gold and took its licence, its Letter of Marque. As they sailed off, 'that Buffoon Toby Thomas by name, said, "Poor Dampier, thy Case is like King James, every Body has left thee"'.†

With two men at the pumps, bailing out, the *St George* continued to cruise. Someone stuffed its holes with tallow and charcoal 'not daring to drive in a Nail, for fear of making it worse'. The four great guns, which stood between decks, were put in the hold. There were no men to manage them and there was no ammunition.

Dampier headed ignominiously for home. The only prize his riff-raff crew now aimed for was life. They had to take a ship in which to sail ten thousand miles across the South Sea. In February they hijacked a Spanish brigantine.* Dampier headed west in it. He abandoned the decrepit *St George* at anchor.

The going was worse than hard. Provisions looted from coastal towns did not last. They drank water thick with duck weed and were rationed to less than half a pound of flour a day per man 'and that very full of Vermine, Maggots and Spiders'. They scalded this concoction with water then ate it. They could not sleep for hunger, so they drank the green water. 'This would satisfie us a little at the present, so that we could slepp; but as soon as we waked, we always found ourselves as hungry as before.'

At Batavia, because Dampier had no commission to show, he was arrested as a pirate and his ship impounded.** He spent more than a year in gaol before being sent back to England at

* A small vessel equipped for both sailing and rowing.
** Batavia is now Jakarta.

the end of 1707 with nothing in his pockets at all.

A handful of other survivors had straggled back. Funnell's party arrived in August 1706 'being but eighteen out of one hundred and eighty-three which went out with us'. They had sailed across the South Sea with no doctor, medicines or carpenter, no anchors, cables, or boat. All their experiences were appalling. They were constantly desperate for water and food. At the island of Guam when they tried to scavenge something to eat, naked men in boats followed them 'menacing at a distance with their Paddles'. They endured gales and monsoon winds: 'the Sea took us a-head, a-stern and on both sides, that we were always almost covered with Water.' At the island of Manipa, colonised by the Dutch, the Governor refused them victuals, starving though they were.

They reached the spice island of Amboyna at the end of May 1705.* The Dutch towed them in and took their vessel. According to Sheltram and Clift, Morgan made ten thousand pounds for himself by selling the silver plate, bullion and jewels he had stolen and hidden away. Those who could not bribe their keepers were interned, badly treated and fed inedible meat. At night they were plagued by mosquitoes. 'We were forced to put ourselves in a Bag, before we could go to sleep.'

At Batavia they met up with some of Clipperton's men. Morgan sold the owners' share of the plunder for £600 then made his own way back to London. Those without money lived off their wits. Survivors were shipped home with the Dutch East India fleet.

For the London owners the adventure was a disaster: both

---

* Amboyna is now Ambon in Indonesia.

ships lost and no booty. Thomas Estcourt had died in 1704 at the age of twenty-three, and willed his estate to his younger sister Elizabeth. She had married a Richard Cresswell. The Cresswells listened to accounts from survivors, like William Sheltram and Ralph Clift, of theft, plunder, mutiny and lawlessness. They suspected fraud and deception, particularly from Dampier and Morgan.

They began litigation that went on for years. They would claim against any treasure Dampier might ever accrue. Those who had sailed with him, condemned him for bad language, drunkenness, mismanagement, dishonesty, and failure to take the rich prizes he promised.[†]

They would Spare no Stranger   1707

ON DAYS when Selkirk did not scan the south side of The Island he feared he might have missed the ship of rescue or the manoeuvres of an enemy sail. High at his lookout above the bay, the air was cool when the valley was humid, there was shade from the *luma* and *gunnera* and the huge ferns. Away from the enclosing valley, he could see the fracture of the archipelago, Santa Clara, the little broken islets, the peaks and ridges of mountains stretching out.

It occurred to him that England might have been defeated in the war, that no friendly ship might again come to these seas, that the whole of the South Sea might now be occupied by Spain. Three times from this vantage point he saw a ship, far out, circle The Island, then traverse the bay from west to east. It was as if it was the same ship. He saw its sails. Each time he ran to the bay. He dragged a burning branch to the shore and stoked a fire until it blazed. The ship sailed by.

Then one dawn he went to the shore's edge and a ship was there. Flying the red and yellow flag of Spain. Anchored in the bay with boats heading in. There were men like him on the shore. For a moment he stared, then turned and ran for the protecting trees.

His retreat was an admission. They pursued him, firing pistols and shouting in Spanish. *Salvaje* he heard, and *perro*. Had they been French he would have surrendered and hoped as a prisoner for transport to Europe. But he would rather die alone on The Island than fall into the hands of the Spaniards. They would murder him or use him as a slave in the silver mines.

Fit as he was, and sure of the terrain, escape was hard. There were many of these men, all armed. They pursued him, shooting, yodelling, as if he were indeed a goat.

He made for thick woodland at the eastern mountain, where he had fashioned a hideout, high in a tree. 'At the foot of the tree they made water, and kill'd several Goats just by, but went off again without discovering him.' He feared they would smell him, sense his presence, flush him out. But they gave up. He was not big game. He was of no more consequence than a wolf or deer that got away.

Again The Island protected him. Its darkness and concealing woodland. At night he drank water, ate birds' eggs and plums, saw other creatures that like himself searched cautiously for sustenance, scrabbled for cover and sniffed at the air.

His enemy stayed two days. Their sounds of departure reached him, then a palpable silence. When he returned to his

glade his lamed kids were dead, the fire out, his hut burned
to the ground. But again he had kept his life and again The
Island, the shimmering sea and the hills.

The Wheeling Terns, the Lumbering Seals

THEY HAD destroyed his sea chest, kettle, bedding, bible and
books, the tools he had forged and nails he had whittled. He
had few possessions when he arrived. They left him with even
fewer.

It was a clear day. Hummingbirds fed on purple flowers
(*Rhaphithamnus venustus*). Shearwater skimmed the sea, on
which for once he was glad that no ship sailed. Cats came out
of the undergrowth mewling. A kitten chased a leaf.

His visitors had left traces: picked bones and footprints
in the sand. He scoured the shore for their debris: a gold coin,
three arak bottles, a rusty anchor, a broken cask, a piece
of sailcloth, a short length of chain, a coil of worn rope, discarded lumber. Their garbage became tools and materials
with which to refurbish his home.

Once again he lit a fire, the long friction of wood on wood.
He improvised a forge. Over days and weeks he hammered
iron, hacked timber, rebuilt his huts, caught goats, herded
kids into a walled enclosure, stored food, rendered seal fat into
tallow, ground ears of corn, wove a basket from twigs, made
string from rope, moulded pots from mud and burned them
hard in the fire. With patience he restored what had been
destroyed.

His new bed was an improvement, raised higher from
the ground. The stone pots he used to cook his food were still

intact, so was the raft from which he sometimes liked to fish. His knife he kept strapped to his side. As a precaution he built another tree house in the mountains, high in the forest on the southern side. An enemy might again arrive.

And so his life resumed, the habits of the day, the intelligence of survival. It occurred to him that there were worse scenarios than rescue. The Island calmed his mind. He had no bible now, but he thanked some notional God who might have brought him to this special place.

The illustrations that follow are of The Island approached from the west (photo Gabriel Perez), the author a thousand feet above sea level and the view from Selkirk's Lookout (photos Pierre Kenyon).

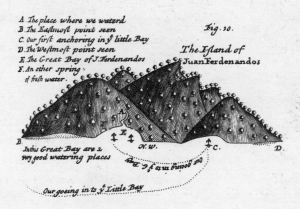

A. The place where we watered
B. The Eastmost point seen
C. Our first anchoring in ye little Bay
D. The Westmost point seen
E. The Great Bay of J. Ferdenandos
F. An other spring
    of fresh water

Fig. 10.

The Island of
Juan Ferdenandos

B.

In this Great Bay are 2
very good watering places

N.W.

C.

D.

Our goeing in to ye Little Bay

God Send them Well

1708

THE FIASCO of Dampier's expedition was a 'great Discouragement' to him. But still the prize glistered, the dream of riches – Diamonds and Gold, the Carpets of Persia, the Silk of China.

He was fifty-six.[†] Affidavits and bitter talk confirmed his ineptitude as a commander. But he could still woo venture capitalists with talk of the Acapulco galleon. He had the credibility of experience. He remained the only living Englishman to have sailed twice round the World. His published journals proved his knowledge of the South Sea.

The ambition of his plan had not been at fault, he said. It was the worm-infested ships, the quarrelsome and incompetent officers, the undisciplined men. There were lessons to heed, but the Spanish treasure galleons still plied the South Sea. Fortune, as ever, was there to be seized.

A syndicate of Bristol councillors financed a new expedition. Three of the backers were erstwhile Mayors. The Sheriff and Aldermen all had a stake. Christopher Shuter put in £3,105. John Romsey, the Town Clerk, put in £1,552, Thomas Goldney, merchant, invested £3,726. Dr Thomas Dover, 'Doctor of Physick', invested £3,312.*

They were encouraged by an Act passed in March 1708 that relinquished the Crown's claim to a share of profits from privateers: 'All Prizes and Purchase which shall be Taken by the said Ships, is to be the sole Use and Benefit of the Owners and Men.'†

They chose Woodes Rogers, a local man, as captain. His father-in-law, Admiral William Whetstone, had commanded the English Caribbean fleet. Rogers had married in 1705, he was a freeman of Bristol, and by 1708 had a house in Queen's Square, three children and social status, but no money. Like Daniel Defoe, he was galled to read that year the journal of a French naval captain, Jacques de Beaucheane-Gouin, that reported profits of £25 million in one year to the French from their activity in the South Sea. Such riches allowed King Louis XIV to continue to finance war with England.

Two frigates, the *Duke* and *Dutchess*, were fitted out, their hulls double-sheathed to deter the awful worms. The *Duke*

---

*Dr Dover was given the sobriquet 'Dr Quicksilver' because he advocated mercury as a remedy for ailments as diverse as infertility and malaria. He claimed a cure for scurvy too – a quarter of a pint of hot milk curdled with potassium and aluminium: 'there needs nothing more to be done for the Cure of this Disease which has hitherto puzzled Physicians of all Ages'.

weighed 320 tons, had 30 guns and cost £6,880, the *Dutchess* weighed 260 tons, had 26 guns and cost £4,160. Both were granted Letters of Marque from Prince George of Denmark, their licence to attack French and Spanish ships in the South Sea.[†]

Rogers was to command the *Duke*, and Stephen Courtney, 'a man of birth, fortune, and of very amiable qualities', the *Dutchess*. Edward Cooke, who like Woodes Rogers kept a journal of the voyage, went as second captain. John Ballett sailed again, accompanied by another surgeon, James Wasse, a 'very honest useful man'. Woodes Rogers' twenty-year-old brother John went as a lieutenant on the *Dutchess*, Joseph Alexander went as linguist, Carleton Vanbrugh, cousin of the architect and playwright, John Vanbrugh, and William Bath went as agents acting in the owners' interests.

Dampier was to be the 'Pilot for the South Seas'. Rogers and Courtney were told that when they rounded the Horn they were 'to consult your pilot Captain Dampier in Counsell on whose Knowledge in those parts we do mainly depend upon for Satisfactory Success'.

Mindful of the chaos of past ventures, the owners drew up meticulous Articles of Agreement. They would pay for ships, artillery ammunition, provisions and charges. The ships were to sail as private Men of War, not Trading Vessels. Two thirds of profits from plunder would go to the owners and a third to the crew. If in battle a Seaman lost a limb or was 'so Disabled as not to get a Livelihood', he would get thirty pounds over and above his respective shares. A Landman would get fifteen. If killed, their widows would get similar sums. If 'any Man shall in Fight or otherwise, Signalize himself, he shall have a farther Reward given him, according to the Bravery of the Action'.

Seventeen investors held a total of two hundred and fifty-six shares. Captains were to get twenty-four shares, Mates and Carpenters six. Ordinary Seamen could choose whether they wanted to be paid in shares of profits, or wages, or a mixture of both ('Twenty Eight Shillings *per Month*, and one share and a Quarter').

All decisions were to be made by a Council of Officers. Money bought executive power. Dr Dover, who held thirty-two shares, had no qualities of leadership and was entirely ignorant of all things nautical, was to be the Council's president.

The crew, as ever, were a rootless lot. There were three hundred and thirty-three of them, of whom only about twenty were sailors:

above one Third were Foreigners from most Nations; several of her Majesty's Subjects on board were Tinkers, Taylors, Hay-makers, Pedlers, Fidlers, &c. one Negro, and about ten Boys. With this mix'd Gang we hop'd to be well mann'd, as soon as they had learnt the Use of Arms, and got their Sea-legs, which we doubted not soon to teach 'em, and bring them to Discipline.[†]

As in 1703, the ships sailed first to the Irish provisioning port of Kinsale. Among supplies taken on board were

four Barrells of Beefe, four Hogsheads of Pork, eighty two ferkins of Butter, six hundred weight of Cheese, Eighteen Butts of Beere, three Boxes of Soape, Fourteen Boxes of Candles, Twelve Barrells of Oatmeale, Three Hogsheads of Vinegar, Six Pieces of Canvas for Hammocks, Fourty Beds, Fourty Pillows and Fourty Rugs, Fiffty Red Coats and one hundred and fifty Capps, Four Casks of Tallow, Six hors hydes and three Sole Leather hydes, one earthen Oven, Twelve dozen Stockings and One hundred weight of Corke.[†]

At Kinsale men 'were continually marrying'. Itinerant lawyers and priests drew up contracts of a dubious sort. A Dane married an Irishwoman though neither could speak a word of each other's language. The men 'drank their Cans of Flip till the last minute' and did not seem to care where they were bound. Agents' letters to the owners voiced alarm that the expedition might not prove as disciplined as envisaged in the Articles of Agreement:

we cannot Express by our pens the fateagues and trouble we have had... It would be endless to relate what has happened... Capt. Rogers Managmt. made ye Matters worse... I hope there will bee more regularity and a better harmony between ym when they gett into deep Water... God send them well, and that they may be Successful to Answer the Vast expence they have beene for you.

Good Order and Discipline   1708

THE SHIPS left Kinsale on 1 September 1708 at ten in the morning. They headed south. They were, said Rogers, 'crouded and pester'd and not fit to engage an Enemy without throwing Provisions and stores overboard.'[†] They needed urgently to take a prize so men could be transferred.

At the first Council Meeting it was agreed that a reward of Twenty Pieces of Eight should go to whoever first glimpsed an enemy sail. This was an encouragement to the men to be observant. It was also a cause of dispute. There was much discussion too about the paucity of liquor on board. The men were 'meanly clad' though the expectation was for the weather to be at times 'excessive cold'. 'Good Liquor to Saylers is preferable to Clothing' Rogers wrote. Dampier spoke highly of the wine from Tenerife, so it was decided to stop there.

On 11 September they chased and took a Swedish ship. Justification for the attack was that it might be carrying smuggled goods, but the charge could not be proved. Sweden had no part in England's conflict with France and Spain. Officers let the ship go. This prompted the boatswain of the *Duke*, Giles Cash, to incite ten men to mutiny. Rogers retaliated with harsh punishment. The culprits were put in irons, guarded by sentries and fed bread and water. Cash was 'soundly whip'd for exciting the rest to join him', then put ashore at Madeira. 'Good Order and Discipline' were to be enforced on this voyage.

Food went fast among so many men. On 18 September near Tenerife they took their first prize – a small Spanish merchant ship with forty-five passengers. Against Rogers' advice, Carleton Vanbrugh went ashore at Tenerife to negotiate a ransom with the Governor. He was promptly detained. Rogers wanted to leave him to rot, but after an exchange of letters he was released with 'Wine, Grapes, Hogs and other Necessaries for the Ransom of the Bark'.

Vanbrugh complained of Rogers' treatment of him. Efforts were made to resolve such grievances at Committee Meetings 'to avoid needless Misunderstandings so early in the Voyage'. Revised clauses to rules were drawn up about punishment for disobeying a superior officer's commands, or for being drunk, or deserting, or about anticipated division of plunder – the most contentious issue.

As the ships pushed toward Cape Horn, hunger and scurvy took lives. The weather was 'excessive cold with violent storms'. The Tailor turned blankets into coats. In a gale with winds of forty knots, the sea washed in through the stern windows of the cabins in the *Dutchess*.* Lieutenant William Stretton was swept down deck with muskets, pistols and the officers' dinner.

The first death from scurvy was recorded on 7 October. Others followed. One Friday a young man, George Davies, fell from the mizzen topsail yard on the quarterdeck and broke his skull. John Ballett bled him, but 'he remained speechless'.

When they crossed the Tropic of Capricorn, first timers were, as ever, ducked in the sea as they clung to a rope hoisted from the yardarm. Rogers thought the ritual 'too Heathen'.

Hardship, boredom and proximity led to fights which the introduction of morning and evening prayers did not prevent. Vanbrugh was transferred to the *Dutchess* the animosity between him and Rogers became so acute. Captain Cooke was hit by his Second Mate, William Page, who as punishment had his feet shackled, was beaten, then confined in irons.

Dampier's memory got worse by the day. He was unsure of the location of the Cape Verde islands and did not remember that he had visited them before. The ships chanced on them at the beginning of October and anchored at St Vincent, desperate for fresh water. The water casks 'stunk insufferably'. The men killed 'monstrous Creatures covered in quills', and spiders the size of walnuts, and bought tobacco, brandy, cows, 'Lemmons, oranges, poultry &c'.

They endured more gales and wet weather as they headed for Le Grande. On 3 December they saw Porpusses and

*Knots are nautical miles per hour.

Grampusses, Seals and 'Great Parcels of Weeds'. The Governor of the island made them welcome and they bartered with him for 'necessaries and Refreshments'. In exchange for women's clothes, bags of snuff and cases of scissors taken from the prize ship, the privateers received thirty-four bulls, rum, sugar, sheep and pigeons.

The men got 'more than half Drunk' and regaled the Governor and a Convent of Fathers with '"Hey Boys up we go" and all manner of Paltry Tunes'. Vanbrugh caused trouble by gratuitously shooting at men in a canoe. He killed a Friar's Indian slave and caused the loss of the canoe's cargo of gold. The Friar said he would 'seek for Justice' in England and Portugal.

At Christmas as they neared the Falkland Islands they saw an albatross, 'who spread its Wings from eight to ten feet wide'. On New Year's Day Rogers ordered a large Tub of Punch to be brewed on the quarterdeck. Each man was poured a pint of it and drank to the ships' owners, Great Britain, a Happy New Year, a good voyage and a safe return.

Liquor did not answer all problems. Fifty men had scurvy. Eight had dysentery. John Veale's legs swelled up. Thomas Rush and Quire Johnson died. 'The Men grow worse and worse and want a Harbour to refresh 'em' Woodes Rogers wrote. All hopes were focused on reaching the haven of Juan Fernandez, but no one was sure of its latitude

the Books laying 'em down so differently, that not one Chart agrees with another; and being but a small Island we are in some doubts of striking it.

A Ship with White Sails 1709

SELKIRK WAS cooking food by his hut in the late afternoon, when the ship of rescue came. He judged the month to be late January. He scanned the sea and there, on the horizon, was a wooden ship with white sails. He knew that it was his ship. It was so much the ship of his dreams.

In the moment of seeing it time stopped. There seemed no interval between the point of abandonment and this promise of rescue. The same wide bay, the straight line of the horizon, the high cliffs and wheeling birds. Nothing had happened between then and now. Only the inchoate process of his mind. Uncommunicated. Lost. He had been nothing to anyone. A shadow of self.

A second ship came into view. It seemed that here again were the *Cinque Ports* and the *St George*. He felt in conflict, fearing the ships would pass, wanting them to pass, fearing the fracture of his solipsism, the sullying of The Island. He supposed that the same men had come back for him, that Stradling was the captain of the smaller vessel. He hated him as acutely as the day they had quarrelled. He would rather die alone in the mountains than see him face to face.

The ships were heading east. He thought they would miss The Island, it was such a small block of land. Even Captain Dampier with his legendary navigational skills had sailed past, supposing it to be somewhere else.

Selkirk dragged a burning log to the beach. It was meant as his beacon of welcome. He wanted to show that his was the bay of safety, that here were warmth, food and water. He wanted to steer his brothers away from the sheer cliff face.

He was with them again. The cold sea air at night, the drenching rains, the misery of sodden clothes. Many he knew would be near death from scurvy and hunger. Like Will before him, he killed three goats, skinned and butchered them and roasted the meat on embers. He gathered turnips and herbs for a soup. Guests were coming to his Island. Rescue was near.

He knew he must not let this ship elude him. Here was a task at which he must not fail. He threw wood on the beach fire until it blazed. He made The Island bright with flames.

1709 *The Light on the Shore*

AT SEVEN in the morning on the last day of January 1709 Woodes Rogers saw a ridge of land, fringed with cloud. It was The Island. Locating it had been hard. Dampier 'was much at a loss', though he said he had a map of it in his head. He had to return to the coast of Chile to get his bearings. The ships sailed east, located Valparaiso, then again headed due west.

Rogers was uncertain of a safe route in to the Great Bay. The wind blew in squalls. Fearing shipwreck against the cliffs, he kept about twelve miles out. At two in the afternoon, Captain Dover took the *Duke*'s pinnace and its crew to explore the shore and find the road into the bay. It was a dangerous distance for a small boat in turbulent waters. By dusk the pinnace was within three miles of the shore. Plying the lee of The Island the men saw Selkirk's fire. They took it as evidence of an enemy. Woodes Rogers dimly saw the fire's light too. At first he thought it to be a signal from the pinnace, but as the sky darkened he decided it was too large for that.

He gave a signal for the boat to return:

We fir'd one Quarter-Deck gun and several Muskets, showing Lights in our Mizen and Fore-Shrouds, that our Boat might find us. About two in the Morning our Boat came on board, having been two hours on board the Dutchess, that took 'em up a-stern of us: We were glad they got well off, because it begun to blow. We are all convinced the Light is on the shore, and design to make our Ships ready to engage, believing them to be French ships at anchor, and we must either fight 'em or want Water &c.

So, because of Selkirk's bonfire, the men prepared to fight. They feared there might even be a Spanish garrison to defeat. They were in dire need of water, food and land. They could not sail on. Dampier advised that they make for the south of The Island, then go in to the bay with the first southerly wind close to the Eastern Shore.

At ten next morning the ships reached the Great Bay. Heavy flaws from the shore forced them to reef their topsails. The *Dutchess* flew a French ensign. They expected sight of the enemy, but there was no sign of human life, or in the next bay, three miles to the west. 'We guess'd there had been Ships there, but that they were gone on sight of us' Rogers wrote.

At noon he sent the yawl ashore with Thomas Dover, Robert Frye and six other men all armed. On the ships all hands were told to stand by the sails, 'for fear of the Winds carrying 'em away'.

Who Was He?   1709

SELKIRK COULD not believe that the pinnace had come so close to the shore, then turned. That his fire of welcome had been misconstrued. It was *déjà vu*: waves breaking against the shore, a boat moving away toward a waiting ship, while he stood powerless at the water's edge. Only this time he was in goatskin and had spoken to no one for four years and four months.

Reason told him they must investigate more and check at dawn for enemy ships. That they would long for a harbour and know there was no other land nearby. But he could not be sure. He saw the lights go out in the Mizzen and Fore-Shrouds and knew the pinnace had returned. He banked the flames of the fire and stared across the starlit water. He saw the ships glide to the east and felt his chance of rescue wane. He would die on The Island as ships passed by.

It was intolerable to do nothing, but he could do no more than wait. If he lit another fire they would assume an enemy. Without a fire, they would not know of his need. He ran to his lookout, up the pass he had carved. He had not slept or eaten for twenty-four hours. At the mountain's ridge, when the sky lightened and the forest clamoured with sounds of life, he stared at the surrounding sea. As ever there was no ship in view. Only a grey sea with a white hem. Cliffs and silence.

Descending the mountain he saw the yawl and its crew. He believed them to be English but he was not sure. The men's stature, the shape of the boat were familiar. He waved a piece of white rag on a stick. The men called to him to show them where to land. He ran to the eastern edge of the shore where the rocks were manageable, the water deep and a boat could be secured. He stood on the rocks. Eight men pointed guns at him. He raised his hands above his head. He tried to speak, he said, 'Marooned.'

He was clearly unarmed, but only because he was on two legs did they think him human. They feared he might be some hybrid of the forest, of a cannibal tribe, a primitive beast like in Dampier's journals, a thing for dissection, or to be put on show. If you left your home and crossed the seas this was the kind of curiosity you found.

They butted him with guns and fired questions. Who was he? Was he alone? Why was he there? What was his name? Where was his ship? He stood with his palms spread and said again, 'Marooned.' He turned his hands to the hut by the shore, the quenched fire, the broth he had prepared for them, the mountains, and then he wept.

The men laughed. Their need was for water and food. They turned their attention to the clear streams, the cooked food, the lobsters that clawed the stones. He showed them The Island's larder, where to bathe under running water, the herbs that were a salve to wounds. Robert Frye went with him over the rocks and through the thickets to the clearing in the mountains where he had built his huts and tamed cats and goats. He showed another man his home.

Absolute Monarch   1709

THE SHIPS stayed outside the bay. The yawl was gone so long Woodes Rogers feared it had been seized. He sent more armed men in the pinnace to investigate. It too disappeared for an unconscionable time. He fired signals for the boats to return

On shore the men quizzed Selkirk. He was a trophy, a curiosity. He became agitated and incoherent. 'He had so much forgot his Language for want of Use, that we could scarce understand him, for he seem'd to speak his words by halves.'

They invited him to the ship. He tried to say he would not

leave The Island if a certain person was on board. They did not know what he meant. He said it again. There was someone whom he could not meet, a man whom he hated, who had consigned him to a living death. He told them it was Stradling, Thomas Stradling. They assured him Stradling was not among the officers, that the only men from the previous journey were William Dampier and John Ballett. He could come with them to the ship and see for himself. If he was not satisfied, they would leave him on The Island.

'Our Pinnace return'd from the shore' Woodes Rogers wrote in his journal, 'and brought abundance of Craw-fish, with a Man cloth'd in Goat Skins who look'd wilder than the first Owners of them.'

Barefoot, hairy and inarticulate, Selkirk boarded the *Duke*. He shook hands with men: Woodes Rogers, William Dampier, Thomas Dover, Carleton Vanbrugh, Alexander Vaughan, Lancelot Appleby, John Oliphant, Nathaniel Scorch. They said his name, welcomed him and put their arms around his shoulders.

Woodes Rogers in particular asked many questions. Where was he from? What voyage had he been with? What was his rank? How had he survived? How long had he been alone? Selkirk found it hard to answer. His thick Fife accent, this overwhelming rescue, the unfamiliar company of men, the incoherence of his punishment, the severance from a place that at times had seemed a paradise...

So he told them what they perhaps wanted to hear. He was Alexander Selkirk. He came from Fife in Scotland. He had been alone on The Island four years and four months. Captain Stradling from the *Cinque Ports* had left him there. He had built a hut of pimento wood, and sandalwood, made a fire, stitched skins for clothes, tamed cats and kids, chased goats, picked little black plums from high in the mountains. He told them of the arrival of the Spaniards and of the day when he fell down the mountain precipice and nearly died. He told them of how, because he was a man, he had survived.

They offered him liquor. It was hard to drink, it so burned his throat. They gave him food so salty he could not eat it. They gave him clothes and he felt constrained, shoes that made his feet swell and which he felt obliged to discard. They arranged his hair and shaved his beard. On Dampier's recommendation, he was appointed Second Mate on the *Duke*.

Woodes Rogers called him the Governor of The Island and its Absolute Monarch. Selkirk could not explain that it was not like that. That The Island had governed him and was its own Monarch. That it would erupt again. That he had been subdued by the enfolding mountains and the unrelenting winds. That the true experience of being marooned was elusive, noumenal, that it was in his eyes perhaps, but not his words. That The Island had cast him in on himself to the point where no time had passed, except for the silence between breaking waves.

The World of Men   1709

SO SELKIRK returned to the world of men. He was The Island's host. He showed his guests its yield, impressed them with its hospitality. He spoke with pride of how verdant it was, how moderate the summer heat and mild the winter, the absence of venomous or savage creatures, the abundance of fish.

He was a guide to the forests of sandalwood and cabbage palm, he taught how to watch for falling trees, landslides and puffins' nests concealed in the earth, which could snare a man and break his leg.

Woodes Rogers saw potential interest in this story of a man marooned on an island, who survived alone through strength and cunning, thrived on temperance and had no use for gold. In a letter to the owners which reached them via sloop and ship and mule and months of time, he wrote of 'Alexander Salcrig',

a Scotchman who was left there by Capt Stradling Capt Dampier's consort the last Voyage and survived four Years and four Months without conversing with any creature, having no Company but wild Goats and his Catt, there being no European in all that Time, and he was resolvd to die alone rather than submitt to ye South Sea Spaniards.[†]

Selkirk displayed his strength. He showed he was not a victim, of Time, or The Island, or of Men. He impressed Rogers with his agility:

He ran with wonderful Swiftness thro the Woods and up the Rocks and Hills. As we perceiv'd when we employ'd him to catch Goats for us. We had a Bull-Dog, which we sent with several of our nimblest Runners, to help him in catching Goats; but he distanc'd and tir'd both the Dog and the Men, catch'd the Goats, and brought 'em to us on his back.[†]

Spare sails, secured to pimento trees, served as tents for the sick. Selkirk fed the ill men with broth of goats' meat, greens and herbs – parsley, purslain, mint and sithes. He strewed their tents with sweet-smelling sandalwood. He gathered plums, boiled and broiled lobsters. Edward Wilts and Christopher Williams died of scurvy, others recovered fast.

The men needed to refit their ships within a fortnight.

They had heard that 'five stout *French* ships were coming together to these Seas'. The peaceful bay became a town. Smiths
and coopers worked by the shore. A group of men slew seals
and boiled up eighty tons of oil 'for the use of our Lamps and
to save our Candles'. They cooked baby seal while they
worked and likened it to the roast lamb of home.

On the ships the decks were cleaned of shit and filth,
smoked to choke out rats and scrubbed with vinegar. Wood
was loaded and water hosed into casks. Turnip tops, herbs
and greens were stored and two hundred large fish salted 'for
future spending'.

Rogers wanted a supply of live meat. Selkirk told him that
from his lookout he had seen herds of large goats grazing in
the south-west lowlands. He could not get to them on foot
across the jagged mountains. Rogers sent him in the *Duke*'s
pinnace with Dampier and twelve other men.

They were gone twenty-four hours. It was Selkirk's first
night away from the Great Bay in four years. He was in the
company of men. They camped on scrubland and got drunk.
They tried to snare a herd of one hundred goats, but most
'escap'd over the Cliff'. They caught sixteen and took them
from the quiet of the hills to the terror of the sea.

The sea beckoned, the desire to snare great fortune. Council Meetings were held about pursuit of prizes and signals for
rendezvous. Detailed codes of communication between the
ships were agreed· the meaning of lights and flags shown, sails
hauled up and down, crosses left at landing places pointing to
messages in glass bottles.

But the issue that rankled was as ever how to share the
booty. It was this, in Rogers' view, that had 'prov'd too hard a

Task for all others in our Time that have gone out on the same account, so far from Great Britain'. Managers of Plunder were elected, with representatives from officers and men. Transparency was assured. Inventories would be kept to include every item seized. All men would be searched as they came from a prize. The focus was again on Gold, Conquest and the Manila Galleon.

1709 *Barnacles off her Bottom*

THEY MOVED from the Great Bay at three in the afternoon on 14 February 1709. A fair wind blew, south, south-east. Selkirk turned between tasks to watch The Island recede. He saw the same as other men: mountains and gorges, sheer cliffs washed by surf, a silhouette of land, a shape, a form.

He had lived in that place for 52 months, or 38,000 hours, or 2,280,000 minutes, or for no time at all. He had left only traces, notches on trees, lamed goats, the embers of a fire, the soul of a marooned man. He took with him a cat, a few stones and images of splendour he could not convey. Soon ferns would cover the huts he had built, his shards of crockery and improvised knives. The seals would grieve their culling then breed again. The fish, goats, trees, all would regenerate as the sun rose over the mountains, as the rains came and the earth turned.

But now there was work to be done of a manly sort. The plan was to voyage north along the coast of Peru, to seize merchant vessels, ransack the port of Guayaquil, then lie in wait near Acapulco until the great prize, the Manila galleon sailed into view.

From the chaos of the *Cinque Ports* and abandonment on The Island, Selkirk was now in the company of strategic thieves. On this voyage men were accountable to officers and disciplined if they broke rules. But still discontent festered, aggravated by boredom, deprivation and inaction: 'Our Men begin to repine that tho come so far we have met with no Prize in these Seas' Woodes Rogers wrote.

After a month of uneventful cruising, they took a small Spanish merchant ship. It was heading toward Cheripe in Peru to buy flour. They used its provisions, held its passengers prisoner and at the Island of Lobos de la Mar, 'a small barren Place having neither wood nor water', refitted it and relaunched it as the *Beginning*. Edward Cooke was appointed its captain. At Lobos too the *Dutchess* was cleaned of 'Barnacles off her Bottom, almost as large as Muscles. A Ship grows foul very fast in these Seas'.† A Dutchman working at this was pulled into the water by a seal and bitten to the bone in several places.

Ten days later, on 26 March, the crew of the *Dutchess* captured another prize, the *Santa Josepha*. It weighed fifty tons and had a cargo of timber, cocoa, coconut and tobacco. It was renamed the *Increase* and used as a hospital ship. All the sick men and two doctors were transferred to it. Selkirk was appointed its Master.

These prizes were useful but inconsequential. They were no reward for the ordeal of the voyage. There were days of roaming the sea when nothing was seen but the spouting of a whale. Scurvy spread and the men's discontent. They were rationed to three pints of water a day per man, for all needs. 'We can't keep the Sea much longer' Woodes Rogers wrote in his journal. On 11 April the Committee 'came to a full

Resolution to land and attempt Guayaquil'. It was a bold ambition. Guayaquil was a rich town, the third largest port of South America. It had an army and a population of two thousand. The men 'began to murmur about the Encouragement they were to expect for Landing, which they alledg'd was a risque more than they were ship'd for'.† Their acquiescence was bought with promises of wine and brandy, of new clothes and a revised share of the prize money.

1709 *Seven Bunches of Garlic and One Very Old Hat*

ON 15 APRIL as they neared Guayaquil, they added a fourth ship and more prisoners to their squadron. They attacked and took a French-built galleon, the *Havre de Grace* as it left the harbour. In the skirmish, Woodes Rogers' brother, John, aged twenty, got shot through the head. He was buried at sea. Prayers for the Dead were intoned and flags flown at half-mast.

'There were upwards of 50 *Spaniards* and above 100 Negroes, *Indians*, and Molattoes on board' Edward Cooke wrote.† Such a crowd was a questionable prize. It consumed food and took up space. Spaniards useful as hostages were listed by name: Sebastian Sanchez, Nicolas Cedillo, Joseph Lopzaga... Negroes and livestock were counted: 2 old Negro women, 3 young Women, 3 Girls, 6 Boyes, 1 young sick Man, 50 young and middle aged Men, 37 Fowls, 7 Sheep, 3 Pigs, 1 Sow and a peck of potatoes.

Selkirk and others made detailed inventories of the ship's booty. These were compared for accuracy. Every item was listed: clothes and silver-handled swords, buckles and snuffboxes, rings and gold chains, a case of bottles and pickles, a chest of chocolate sweetmeats, a black box of odd things, 1 pair of spectacles, 7 bunches of garlic, 1 very old hat, 5 muslin Neckcloths, 1 white Cap, 1 very little box with bells and brass Nayles, 1 wig.*

Things thought worthless were dumped overboard. Among these were beads and crucifixes, wooden effigies of the Virgin Mary, thirty tons of papal medals, bones in small boxes 'ticketed with the names of Romish saints, some of whom had been dead for 7 or 800 years' and 500 bales of papal dispensations to eat meat during Lent if the appropriate fee was paid.† About a hundred of these bales were kept back. Like the thatches of villagers' houses, they were used to burn off barnacles when careening the ships.

The *Havre de Grace* was refitted as a companion to the *Duke* and *Dutchess*. It was given new masts, sails and rigging and renamed the *Marquess*. The chief Gunner of the *Duke* transported arms to it in a frigate: twenty guns, gun carriages, shot and nails, hand grenades, powder horns, shells, crowbars and cutlasses. Edward Cooke was put in command with a crew of ninety men.

Intercepted letters on the ship showed the Spanish authorities knew about the privateers. The Viceroy, the Marquis de Castelldosrius, had written to all the *Corregidors* of the South American coastal towns. He warned them to guard their ports, shores and harbours, deny all provisions to the English, and be prepared for surprise attack.

---

*Woodes Rogers bought this wig for £7.

1709 *Take 'em off and Surrender 'em*

THE PRIVATEERS planned sudden and stealthy invasion of Guayaquil. Two hundred and one of them lurked in barks in the mangrove swamps. They were armed with quarterdeck guns, field carriages and pistols. They had with them seven high-ranking Spanish prisoners as hostages. One hundred and fifty other prisoners had been left in leg irons on the ships.

The uncertain strategy was to land in three convoys commanded by Thomas Dover, Woodes Rogers and Stephen Courtney. There was an officer for every ten men. Dampier was to manage guns and provisions. An Indian pilot who got drunk was 'severely whipt before the whole Company as a Terror to the rest'.[†] The weather was hot, the barks overcrowded and the waters infested with alligators. The men were 'pester'd and stung grievously by Muskitoes'.[†]

On the night of 22 April the people of Guayaquil held a party high on a hill, with fires, bells and gun blast. Rogers construed the commotion as bellicose and wanted immediately to attack. Dampier wanted to return to his ship.

At a hasty and fractious meeting the officers voted to attempt to negotiate with the town's *Corregidor* before invading. Two prisoners were sent to him as envoys with ransom demands. He must pay 50,000 Pieces of Eight to secure the release of prisoners held by the privateers and to avert attack on his town. If he detained the envoys for more than an hour, his town would be ransacked and the prisoners killed.

The *Corregidor* came to the shore with a translator. He asked for time to discuss with his officials the size of the ransom and its method of payment. He agreed to return at eight

that night. The scene was set for his reappearance. A boat
waited for him. On the *Duke* a candlelit table was laid. But he
did not show up. Rogers suspected trickery and wanted to invade the town. Then at midnight an envoy arrived with gifts
of bags of flour, dead sheep and pigs, wine and brandy and a
message that the *Corregidor* would return at seven next morning. Rogers sent a reply: if he failed to show up the ransom
offer was at an end.

The *Corregidor* prevaricated and consulted. There was
barter and threat. The English lowered their demand to
40,000 Pieces of Eight to be paid in nine days. The Spaniards
protested that the price was too high. Time passed.

So we sent our Linguist and a Prisoner with our final Answer, that if they
did not in half an hour send us three more good Hostages for the 40,000
Pieces of Eight agreed on, we would take down our Flag of Truce, land,
and give no Quarter, and fire the Town and Ships.

The Spaniards waved a white handkerchief. They would
parley again. They offered 32,000 Pieces of Eight. They
could not afford more.

Rogers lowered the white Flag of Truce, raised the English Ensign, and ordered his men to invade. At this point all
semblance of discipline and restraint among the men ended.
They 'could be kept under no Command as soon as the first
Piece was fired' he wrote. The Spaniards confronted them on
horseback. The English shot at them, loading and firing very
fast. Twenty Spaniards and as many horses were killed or
wounded.

The English marched to the church of St Jago, ransacked
the houses in the square and set them on fire. Some of these

houses were tall and built of brick, most were timber, the simplest were bamboo huts. They blazed all night and all the following day.

This army was a marauding mob. They looted gold and silver from the church then hoisted the English flag on its tower. They wanted to rip up the floorboards 'to look among the Dead for Treasure'. For reasons of hygiene Rogers opposed this. A contagious epidemic of 'malignant fever' had killed hundreds of Guayaquil's citizens. An open pit was filled with their half-putrefied corpses. The church floor was crammed with recent graves.

To escape the twin evils of epidemic and invasion, the town's citizens had fled to the surrounding hills. The English torched and looted their empty houses and the smaller churches of St Augustin, St Francis, St Dominic and St Ignatius. They ransacked storerooms. They stole silver and clothing, peas, beans, rice, 15 jars of oil, 230 pounds of flour, 160 jars of wine and brandy, a ton of pitch, irons, nails, cordage, guns, indigo and cocoa, a ton of loaf sugar and the *Corregidor*'s gold-headed cane.[†]

An Indian prisoner told Rogers of safe houses up river where most of the town's women and a great deal of money had been taken. Selkirk and John Connely were given charge of twenty-one men and sent in a boat with 'a Cask of good Liquor' to flush these women out.

They broke into their supposedly safe houses with crowbars. In one they found huddled a group of upper-class Spanish women. Rogers gave his version of what happened:

Some of their largest Gold Chains were conceal'd and wound about their Middles, Legs and Thighs, etc, but the Gentlewomen in these hot

Countries being very thin clad with Silk and Fine Linnen, and their Hair dressed with Ribbons very neatly, our Men by pressing felt the Chains etc with their Hands on the Out-side of the Lady's Apparel, and by their Linguist modestly desired the Gentlewomen to take 'em off and surrender 'em. This I mention as a Proof of our Sailors Modesty, and in respect to Mr Connely and Mr Selkirk, the late Governour of Juan Fernandoes.

So Woodes Rogers claimed in his edited journal. These men, who had been at sea for eight frustrating months and, in Selkirk's case, marooned alone for four and a half years, who could not be controlled 'as soon as the first piece was fired', who had drunk a good deal of liquor, smashed their way into churches with iron crowbars and torched people's houses, none the less when it came to sexual civility, defied the customs of war and behaved with modesty and respect as they groped women's bodies to steal their jewels.

They stripped them of gold chains, earrings and jewels to the value of a thousand pounds. Then they moved on to other houses where there were other women. When they returned down river they called again on 'these charming prisoners'.

The Spaniards pleaded with the English to leave. They could not defend this town. They offered 30,000 Pieces of Eight and all that had been looted, in return for their barks and hostages. They gave an assurance of payment in twelve days. Rogers told them they would see the whole town on fire if they did not pay up in six.

The Spaniards conceded defeat. An Agreement was signed. The English marched to their boats 'with Colours flying'. Rogers picked up many 'Pistils, Cutlashes and Pole-axes, which shewed that our Men were grown very careless, weak and weary of being Soldiers and that 'twas time to be gone from hence'.

The air was humid and dense with mosquitoes. The soldiers were fatigued. It was hard for them to drag their guns out of the mud to the boats. Sixty men hoisted them to their shoulders on a bamboo frame then waded to the boats through the swamps. They sailed away on 28 April with Drums, Trumpets and Guns and 'Shew and Noise'. The citizens of Guayaquil returned to what was left of their town.

1709 A Melancholy Time

IT WAS a Pyrrhic victory for the privateers. John Martin had been killed by a shell, which split as he fired it from a mortar. Lieutenant William Stretton's pistol went off and shot him in the leg. In the dark a watchman shot Hugh Tidcomb who could not give the password. John Gabriel, a Dutchman, became paralysed with drink and passed out in a Spaniard's house. And within days, one hundred and forty men were sick with high fevers and rasping thirsts. Rogers thought they had 'contagious Distemper', caught from the corpses in the Guayaquil churches. Probably they had malaria.

It was a 'melancholy Time'. There were not enough medicines to attempt a cure. The men died, despite the efforts of John Ballett and James Wasse, who bled them and dosed them with alcohol and spices: Samuel Hopkins, the apothecary, who had read prayers every day, Thomas Hughes, 'a very good sailor', George Underhill, twenty-one and good at mathematics, John English, Laurence Carney, Jacob Scrouder, Edward Donne, Peter Marshall, Paunceford Wall...

Rogers heard that '7 stout Ships well mann'd' were near. He stranded more prisoners in a boat, then sailed north. There was acrimony among the officers about the attack on Guayaquil. Rogers accused Carleton Vanbrugh of having stayed on ship to eat his dinner '& so to avoid by delay the Danger, by landing after the others'. Vanbrugh said Rogers 'turn'd his back on ye Enemy ... under some sham Pretences of our mens being like to shoot him in the Back &c'.[†]

Nor did the purloined provisions last. There was soon a desperate shortage of fresh water, the bread and biscuit were 'so full of Worms that it's hardly fit for Use', rats ate the flour. 'We are so weak' Woodes Rogers wrote in June,

that should we meet an Enemy in this Condition, we could make but a mean Defence. Everything looks dull and discouraging, but it's vain to look back or repine in these Parts.[†]

Thus the life of conquest, the power and glory of slaughter, the pillage, arson, rape and bluster of war. On Selkirk's Island it was autumn and leaves turned gold.

Loathsome Negroes, Whips and Pickles   1709

THE *Duke*, *Dutchess* and *Marquess* cruised on, taking prizes and plunder as they could. The lists grew long of worldly goods accrued: From a ship called the *St Philippe* they purloined one dozen silver buttons, a Woman's black Vale, one red silk petticoat, one old frock, one old quilt, two ladles, three Spindles, one old good-for-nothing Shirt, a pouch of fishing tackle, a brass pan, a bag of potatoes, a prick of tobacco, four pairs of drawers and a map book.

The Spaniards, 'after they knew the English were in ye Seas', embargoed all ships from carrying money, valuables or provisions. For the privateers, meagre rations led to pilfering and punishment. Two who stole water were 'whipped and pickled' – salt and vinegar was rubbed into their open weals. The storeroom steward on the *Duke* slept with the door key tied to his penis. A light-fingered thief got it off him and took bread and sugar. He was 'severely whipt at the Geers and put in Irons'.

And still the men dreamed of the Manila ship and feared it would pass unseen. The intention was to careen the ships at the Galapagos Islands in readiness for this big fight. But Dampier, 'our Pilot', could not locate them. He missed them by 300 miles then would not admit his mistake. 'Capt. Dampier has been here, but it's a long Time ago' Woodes Rogers wrote.

On 13 June, the ships stopped at Gorgona Island. Monkeys and baboons were shot and cooked as fricassees and broth. 'Capt Dampier says he never eat any thing in London that seemed more delicious to him than a Monkey or Baboon.' Seven black prisoners ran into the snake-infested woods, in preference to shipboard life with their masters. One got bitten on the leg by a small speckled snake and died within twelve hours. Another was caught, hauled back to the ship and put in leg irons. He broke free, swam to the shore and hid again. John Edwards 'died of a Complication of Scurvey and the Pox which he got from a loathsome Negro', who was then given to the prisoners, 'that she might do no further Mischief on board'.

Another loathsome Negro 'was deliver'd of a Girl of a tawny Colour' assisted by the midwifery skills of James Wasse and a quantity of Peruvian wine.

To prevent the other she Negro (call'd Daphne) from being debauch'd in our Ship I [Woodes Rogers] gave her a strict Charge to be modest, with Threats of severe Punishment, if she was found otherwise. One of the Dutchess's black Nymphs having transgressed this Way was lately whip'd at the Capston.

In an effort to ward off diverse mutinies and quell cabals, protests and rebellions, shares of plunder were made. The men were given clothes, silver-handled swords, buckles and snuffboxes, rings and gold chains. Such handouts only temporarily assuaged. Resentment at officers being accorded ten shares more than ordinary seamen led to more trouble. Mutineers threatened to take over the *Marquess*, load it with plunder from the *Dutchess*, and let officers like Thomas Dover and Stephen Courtney 'goe to ye Divell'.

They swore God dam them thare should bee noe more Comittees nor Councell. Hee that had ye Longest sword should carray it. And his woard should be ye Law. †

There were too many offenders to punish in chains. Co-operation was bought with further adjustments to the percentage division of spoils.

A Little World Within Itself

1709

SELKIRK TOOK no part in intrigues and feuds. He carried out all tasks assigned to him. He knew the distinction between a share of plunder and dispossession. And he knew to avoid the punishment that could ensue from rebellious display. He had survived The Island, he intended to survive the voyage home.

The privateers chanced on the Galapagos Islands on 10 September 1709. They saw daunting craters, and mountains rising to 4000 feet. Simon Hatley, Third Mate on the *Duke*, went with four others in a prize bark to search for fresh water. He disappeared and did not respond to guns and lights. Selkirk was sent in a boat to look for him. He soon returned. Whatever Hatley's fate, he did not want it for himself.*

The men crammed all available boats with giant tortoises (*Testudo nigra*), creatures that liked to wallow in mud, gulp great quantities of water and feed on succulent cacti, pale green lichen, leaves and berries.

It took eight men to lift a particularly large one, that weighed seven hundred pounds. They hacked it out of its shell, then ate it stewed 'but the Flesh never boils tender'. It yielded two hundred pounds of meat. Stacked on their backs, the tortoises stayed alive depressingly long. They laid eggs on the ships' decks 'about the bigness of a Goose's Egg, white with a large thick shell'. †

One hundred and twenty years after the *Duke* and *Dutchess*, a young British naturalist, Charles Darwin, went with HMS *Beagle* on a surveying voyage round the world. He collected, observed and tried to interpret the flora, fauna and rocks that he found. His expedition took five years and covered 40,000 miles.

The Galapagos Islands, with their endemic species, held for him quintessential proof of evolution. He observed the giant tortoises, the thirteen kinds of finches, the hawks, owls, flycatchers, lizards and guanos. Why, he wondered, did finches and tortoises show variation from island to island, so that it

*Hatley and his companions were captured by the Spaniards, tortured, starved, and put in the same Lima prison as Stradling. They were not freed until peace came in 1713.

was possible to tell which particular island a tortoise came from. It seemed to him that species might share a common ancestor. He saw each island as 'a little world within itself where we are brought near to that great fact – that mystery of mysteries – the first appearance of new beings on this earth'.

'We may be all netted together' he wrote. Common to all living things was the struggle to survive. Nature was mutable and the past and present interdependent:

This wonderful relationship between the dead and the living will, I do not doubt, throw more light on the appearance of organic beings on our earth and their disappearance from it than any other class of facts.[†]

No such sense of affinity to the past or present afflicted the privateers. Their guiding creed was plunder. They ate the alien hares, turtle doves, guanos, parrots and pigeons. They tormented the tortoises and complained of their taste. 'These Creatures are the ugliest in Nature' Rogers wrote. But with rough curiosity, he too wondered how they had arrived on the Islands: 'because they can't come of themselves, and none of that sort are to be found in the Main.' The trumpeter of the *Dutchess* and another man rode around on the back of a particularly large one, for a bit of fun.

Crack a Commandment   1709

WOODES ROGERS did not want to fight the Manila galleon with 'crowded and pestered' ships. He had too many 'Useless Negroes' on board. They ate food and took up space. Those useful as slaves or drudges, or desirable for sex, were kept. Others were herded together to be traded for provisions. Edward Cooke and Edward Frye, who with Woodes Rogers' brother John had fought the *Marquess* 'when in the Hands of the Spaniards', were as their reward given 'the Black Boy Dublin and the Black Boy Emmanuel' to use as they liked.†

'Mr *Selkirk*'s Bark was cleared to carry our Prisoners to the Main, who, being 72 in Number, were very chargeable to maintain.'† Selkirk took them in the *Increase* to Tacames, a remote bay with a tiny village. Two pinnaces with armed men escorted him. The useless Negroes were sold. It was Selkirk's task to discard them on yet another unfamiliar shore. He returned with payment of black cattle, hogs, goats, limes and plantains.

The Padre of the *Marquess* was also put ashore and given

as he desir'd, the prettiest young Female Negro we had in the Prize with some Bays, Linnen and other thing. He parted with us extremely pleas'd and leering under his Hood upon his black Female Angel. We doubt he will crack a Commandment with her, and wipe off the Sin with the Church's Indulgence.

Many commandments were cracked on this voyage round the world. Piety was not at its core.

The little squadron sailed north for Cape St Lucas, at the southern tip of California. There the privateers were to watch and wait for the Manila ship 'whose wealth on board her we hope will prompt every Man to use his utmost Conduct and Bravery to conquer'. It was at St Lucas that Thomas Cavendish in November 1587 had captured the *Santa Ana*, loaded with silks and damasks and gold.

November passed and most of December. The ships cruised the coast without a glimpse of the longed-for prize. The men became 'melancholy and dispirited'. The boredom was terrible. Day after day of the waste of the ocean. No

comfort on the ships. No point to this life. For Selkirk it was a
familiar theme: 'The scarlet shafts of sunrise but no sail.' He
was inured to empty time passing. To the elusiveness of the
imagined ship. But the less hardened men measured the days
by their impatience. They gave up hope and were eager to
head home:

Computing our poor stock of Provisions left, we found there was no pos-
sibillity of continuing the Cruise any longer, but an absolute Necessity of
getting into a Harbour to Refitt, and be gone for the Indies with all Expedition imaginable. Wch being agreed upon, we began to reflect heavily on
our Misfortunes.†

At a Council Meeting on 20 December the men voted to sail
east, without delay, to the Island of Guam and then to the
Indies and home. Their fear was that if they could not reach
Guam in good time, or if they lost their way, or met with danger or hostility, with such scant supplies as they had, they
could not survive. Morale was at its lowest ebb. This voyage
was another failure. The best that could be hoped for was to
return home alive and defeated, a mission unaccomplished,
devoid of glory, with nothing to show for hardship endured.

    And then at about nine in the morning on 21 December,
amid preparations for the voyage home, 'to our great and
joyful Surprize', the man at the masthead cried out that he saw
a sail. It was the Manila galleon, the treasure ship they had all
'so impatiently waited for and despair'd of seeing'.

Tanbes, Sannoes and Charroadorees   1709

THE SHIP of their desperation was called *Nuestra Senora de la
Encarnacion Disengano*. Dampier put its value at a million

pounds sterling. It was a frigate of 400 tons with 20 cannons, 20 small guns, and 193 men on board. Its commander, Jean Pichberty, was brother-in-law of the French Governor in Spain. Its crew thought themselves near the end of a gruelling eight-month journey. To avoid devastating easterly winds they had sailed far north into freezing waters. They were weak from scurvy, cold, and lack of food.

There was no liquor left on the *Duke*, *Dutchess* or *Marquess*. The men were primed for battle with drinking chocolate and prayers. Hunger and hardship made them a determined enemy. This was the prize they would die to take. This was why they were 7000 miles from home, on starvation rations in a shit-encrusted, rat-infested tub.

All day of 21 December and all through that night the *Duke* closed on its prey. The intention was to board it at dawn. To defend itself the *Disengano* hung barrels filled with explosives from each yardarm. The *Duke* and *Marquess* began to bombard it at eight in the morning. The *Dutchess* could not get near – there was not enough wind. The battle lasted three hours. 'The Enemy fired her Stern Chase upon us first', Woodes Rogers wrote,

which we return'd with our Fore Chase several times, till we came nearer, and when close aboard each other, we gave her several Broadsides, plying our Small Arms very briskly, which they return'd as thick a while but did not ply their great Guns half so fast as we. After some time we shot a little ahead of them, lay thwart her Hawse close aboard, and plyed them so warmly that she soon struck her Colours two thirds down. By this time the *Dutchess* came up, and fired about 5 Guns with a Volley of Small Shot, but the Enemy having submitted, made no Return.

On the *Disengano*, twenty men were killed, wounded by gunfire or 'blown up and burnt with Powder'. On the *Duke*,

Woodes Rogers was shot in the face by a musket ball 'in att my Mouth, and out att my left Cheek'. Part of his upper jaw and several of his teeth fell out on deck. In the night he swallowed a lump of jawbone clogged in his throat. The only other casualty among the privateers was an Irishman, William Powell, who got wounded in his bottom.

So, with what were considered light casualties, the galleon was taken. It was only the second time in 120 years that the English had achieved this feat. The *Disengano*'s cargo was of gold dust, gold plate and coins, spices, musk, becswax and textiles. Among its china was a service for Queen Maria Luisa of Spain. There were calicos, chintzes and silks, 5,806 fans, 1084 pairs of cotton stockings and 37 silk gowns. There were quantities of ploughshares and shoes for mules. There were oil paintings of the Virgin Mary, jars of sugar candy, a chest of priests' vestments, Spanish coconuts, tanned goatskins, handbells and bugles, old books, a large looking glass, pictures, snuffboxes, pontificals for the new Archbishop of Lima, and a supply of tanbes, sannoes, charroadorees, palampores, paunches, mulmuls, humhums, nucaneas, sooseys and basts and 'several parcels of odd things'.[†] Such were the treasures of the material world, the stuff of avarice and endeavour, the reward for the fight.

The privateers were elated by this haul, but not satisfied. Interrogation of the captain and officers of the *Disengano* revealed they had sailed from Manila in consort with a bigger ship, with a greater cargo, from which they had separated three months previously. Desiring the bigger, better and other prize, the men, inspired by their success, prepared themselves to pursue that too.

1709 *A Brave Lofty New Ship*

THE OTHER ship, the 'great ship', was twice the size. It was called *Nuestra Senora de Begona* and was on its maiden voyage.* Newly built in the Philippines, it had two decks, weighed nine hundred tons and could blast twelve-pound iron cannon balls from forty brass guns. Its captain Don Fernando de Angulo had a skilled master-gunner and an experienced crew of four hundred and fifty men, many of whom were English or Irish freebooters, with personal stashes of plunder to defend.

On Christmas Day two sentries from the *Duke*, posted on a hill off Cape St Lucas 'made 3 waffs'. They had sighted the second galleon. The *Dutchess* and *Marquess* closed in for a day and a night. At dawn on 27 December they bombarded the *Begona* with bullets, grapeshot, stones and cannon balls. In an eight-hour battle they damaged its rigging and mizzenmast, killed eight of its crew and wounded more.†

The Spanish response was slow but lethal. They had put netting round their decks to prevent the enemy from boarding. Their gunners were concealed 'there being not a Man to be seen above-board'. From out of sight they lobbed fireballs, stink bombs and flaming grenades onto the decks of the English ships and smashed them with cannon balls.

The *Duke* arrived late on the scene. The prior agreement had been for it to separate and close in later, but then there was no wind. It got caught in the *Dutchess*'s fire:

those Shot that miss'd the Enemy flew from the *Dutchess* over us and

---

*Begona was a pilgrim shrine in northern Spain.

betwixt our Masts, so that we ran the risque of receiving more Damage from them than from the Enemy.

There were only one hundred and twenty men capable of fighting on all three English ships 'and those but weak, having been very short of Provisions a long time'. 'The Enemy's was a brave lofty new Ship.' Five hundred six-pound cannon balls did little damage to the *Begona* which blew up the foremast and gunpowder room of the *Dutchess* killing or injuring twenty men. It wrecked the rigging of the *Marquess* and smashed holes in its hull. It lobbed four fireballs on to the quarterdeck of the *Duke*, which destroyed the main mast, blew up a chest of arms and boxes of cartridges, and badly burned Carleton Vanbrugh (the owners' agent) and a Dutchman. Thirty-three other men were killed, wounded, or scorched with gunpowder. Woodes Rogers had his left heel blown off, Thomas Young, a Welshman, lost one of his legs and Thomas Evans's face was 'miserably torn'.

The privateers could not win this battle. They were outclassed in tactics and the Philippine ship was better built than any of theirs. The *Marquess* had three and a half feet of seawater in its hold, 'wch we soon stopd' Edward Cooke wrote, 'and freed our selves and Knotted and Splised our Rigging and was bearing downe againe to the Enemy when we saw the Duke with a Signall out to speak with us.'

He immediately went with Stephen Courtney in a pinnace and boarded the *Duke*:

where we found Capt. Rogers wounded in ye foot by a Splinter with severall of his Men blowne up with the powder and his Main mast Shot through and found them all desirous not to engage the Enemy any farther and we not being able to Engage her by our Selves so left off the Chase ...

we having 27 Men killed and wounded and our Foremast shot through the heart in four places our Mainmast shot through in 2 places, our Mizen mast shot through in 2 places, the whole of our foretopmast shot away with our foretrestle trees and our Main yard Shot through &c.

'We might as well' he wrote, 'have fought a Castle of 50 Guns as this Ship.'

So the Manila galleon sailed on to Acapulco its masts standing, its guns still out, its treasure defended and flying the Armada battle flag. The privateers had to make do with the smaller ship, the lesser prize. Rogers, shot to pieces, doubted if it was all worth the cost: 'This Prize is very Rich but that nor anything else comes near the Unknown Risques and many Inconveniences we have and must Endure.'

They renamed their prize the *Batchelor*, after John Batchelor, a Bristol Alderman and linen draper, one of the owners. The officers quarrelled over who should command it on the journey home. Rogers opposed the election of Thomas Dover as its captain: 'His Temper is so violent, that capable Men cannot well act under him, and himself is uncapable' he wrote.[†] Dover, in retaliation, called Rogers a dead weight, scornful, belligerent and swelled with pride. 'His Sole Business has been to promote discord amongst us. But what can be Expected from a man yt will begin & drink ye Popes health.'[†]

Selkirk was appointed the *Batchelor*'s Master. He had proved himself a capable man and would navigate the ship of fortune on its 19,000-mile voyage home. He did not provoke these fractious captains who blamed each other but not themselves. The value of the plunder would not be known until it was sorted in London. He, like Dampier, supposed it to be a million pounds. He was entitled to a two and a half share.

Enough to give him cloths of gold. The Island without men and money was gone from sight. The unheard echoes in its mountains. The unseen shadows of evening. He had moved from that invisible world to victory in battle, rank on board ship and to the promise of material wealth, and all that such wealth entailed.

The Journey Home   1710

AND SO BEGAN the long haul home. There was no delight now in moonlit nights or white sails filled with a gentle wind. The adventure was over. The sea was a tedious desert of water. Day after day after day. The men wanted comfort, and their share of the booty. 'Itt went very hard with many of us for want of Provisions' Woodes Rogers wrote.

The Manila Galleon though stuffed with riches was scant on stores. Supplies on all ships were rationed: a pound and a half of flour between five men if they were white, or between six if they were black. The men traded rats among themselves for fourpence or sixpence depending on size 'and eat them very savourly'. When Pieces of Pork were stolen, the thieves were thrashed with a cat o' nine-tails. 'A Negro we named Deptford' died of his punishment. Life was no better than death and one man's demise was another's bread.

On the 18th [January] we threw a Negro overboard, who died of a Consumption and Want together... On the 25th Thomas Williams, a Welch Taylor, died; he was shot in the Leg at engaging the 2nd Manila Ship, and being of a weak Constitution, fell into a Dysentery, which kill'd him... The Spanish Pilot we took in the *Batchelor* died; we kept him, thinking he might be of use to us, if he recover'd of his Wounds; but he was shot in the Throat with a Musket-ball which lodg'd so deep, the Doctors could not come at it... On March the 3rd we buried a Negro call'd Augustine, who died of the Scurvy and Dropsy.

And so it went on. The *Duke* 'began to make much Water' which had constantly to be pumped. Rogers could not walk because of his injuries, and had to be hoicked around in a chair. Dampier was vague about the route, and had forgotten landmarks.

They reached the island of Guam on 11 March. It looked green and pleasant. The Spaniards had planted it with melons, oranges and coconuts. Rogers, Courtney and Cooke sent the Governor a letter asking to buy 'Provisions and Refreshments' and promising, were their request refused, 'such Military Treatment as we are with ease able to give you'.

The Governor complied. In exchange for twenty yards of scarlet cloth, six pieces of cambric, nails, religious arte-facts and two Negro Boys dress'd in Liveries, he parted with eight calves and cows, four bullocks, sixty pigs, ninety-nine chickens, twenty-four baskets of corn, fourteen bags of rice, forty-four baskets of yams, eight hundred coconuts and an unspecified number of limes and oranges. His superiors in Manila, when they heard of his hospitality, viewed it as treachery, and put him in prison.

From Guam to the East Indies was another four long months. The going was slow and tedious and the men were again soon thirsty and hungry, Rogers was thin and in crip-pling pain, the *Duke* leaked non stop, the pumps were continu-ally manned, an April gale damaged all ships, and Dampier did not know the way between the myriad islands of the Moluccas.

On 20 June they reached 'the long desired Port of Batavia'. It was in Dutch territory, and the Dutch were allies. It was a city of canals and suburban houses with neat gardens. It spoke of civilisation. Rogers compared it to Bristol. There was abundant food, with luxuries like butter. It seemed that the perils of the sea were over. Rogers sent the good news to the Bristol owners:

Having two prizes in our Company, of wch one is the lesser Manila Ship whom wee took on ye 22 December last off the coast of California We are in good health & are making all Convenient despatch hence, we hope the same good providence which has hitherto so wonderfully preserved & protected us will continue it and Conduct us to a happy meeting wth you and Enjoyment of the Effects of our labours & many risques.[†]

In the relative comfort of a hospital, Rogers had a large lump of musket shot cut out of his jaw. It had been there six months:

we reckon'd it a Piece of my Jaw-bone, the upper and lower Jaw being much broken, and almost closed together, so that the Doctor had much ado to come at the Shot, to get it out. I had also several Pieces of my Foot and Heel-bone taken out.[†]

The privateers stayed four months at Batavia. Their ships needed radical refitting and careening. Javanese caulkers helped with the work. The *Marquess*, when heeled over, revealed 'the bottom being eat to a Honey-Comb by the Worms'. It was sold as salvage, and its cargo divided among the other three ships.* Edward Cooke returned to the *Dutchess* as second captain.

Though there was plenty to eat, the sun's heat was a

*Captain Opey, sailing with an English East India ship, bought it then sold it to Chinese traders for breaking up.

hazard. Five men died of dysentery and yellow fever. A crew-man was torn to death by a shark while swimming. More than seventy men had died on the voyage. Those who had made it thus far drank arak at eight pence a gallon and bought sugar for a penny a pound.

1711 *Great Jarring Among Us*

THE BRISTOL owners wanted their prize home and the plun-der in their pockets. A flurry of letters from Batavia filled them with alarm. The mood among officers and crew was deadly, laced with suspicion, threat and greed. Carleton Vanbrugh told them 'We have had great Jarring among us.' He described Woodes Rogers as a 'Villainous Defamator' who had abused him throughout the entire voyage. Thomas Dover wrote that Rogers was 'disposeing of wt He thinks fitt out of this Ship' and had threatened to cut the throat of any-one who complained. Rogers reminded them he had been promised 'a two and thirtieth part of the whole' at the outset of the enterprise, and warned them to keep to this. 'For Christs Sake don't lett me be torn to pieces at home after I have been so rackt abroad.'[†]

The owners replied that discord would lead to the over-throw of the voyage, that orders and directives must be observed and offenders punished as mutineers.

No precise inventory of the *Batchelor*'s cargo could be drawn up until it was unloaded. Rogers warned them that much might be spoiled. 'We have not yet seen the Goods stowd in the Manila ships hold,' he wrote. 'I wish it might rise out of her free from Damadge.'[†] He put the cargo's value at

£200,000 'separate from all Dutys and Charges'. The crew, always on the edge of mutiny, and rightly suspicious of their officers, valued it at three million pounds and more. They accused Rogers of hiding treasure at Batavia, with the intention of picking it up later.

The plan was for the refitted *Duke*, *Dutchess* and *Batchelor* to sail from Batavia to the Cape of Good Hope and wait there for an escort of Dutch and English warships to take them to Holland. The fear was that without such protection the enemy might seize the prize as it sailed near the coast of north Africa and Spain.

In three more months at sea they made good speed. On 3 and 4 December they covered 270 miles. They arrived at Cape Town on 29 December and anchored in the bay below Table Mountain. Again they were in a friendly town with all the food and drink they desired. To buy 'Necessaries and Provisions like Carrots, Eggs and a suitable Quantity of Rack', Rogers sold one hundredweight of silver plate, sixty ounces of unwrought gold, sundries, and fourteen Negroes. A Negro Woman and her Child fetched £3 10s, a Boy went for £26 5s, and nineteen dozen pairs of European silk stockings went for £56 10s 6d.[†]

The surgeon James Wasse died at the Cape. So too, to Rogers' satisfaction, did Carleton Vanbrugh, badly burned in the battle with the Manila galleon. Edward Cooke arranged his funeral 'the Ships firing Guns every half minute as is customary on these occasions'. He was buried in a Dutch cemetery.

The jarring captains sent more discordant letters to Bristol. Courtney said the *Dutchess* was 'a very sickly ship' and that he and forty of its crew were ill. Rogers described himself as 'just recovered from ye Jaws of death almost' and expressed concern that his share of the treasure should 'make some Amends for what's past'. And Dover and Dampier wrote of how, when they tried to imprison Woodes Rogers for stealing a chest of pearls, jewels and gold, he threatened to kill them.[†]

After three tense months, an escort of sixteen Dutch and nine British warships arrived. The convoy of twenty-eight ships set sail on 6 April commanded by Admiral Pieter de Vos. It was a warlike spectacle and a disciplined manoeuvre, the galleon guarded, all cannon ready. It spoke of victory, triumph and riches. Nothing now was left to chance or luck.

This squadron sailed north over the Atlantic Ocean. Cooke filled sixteen pages of his journal with lists of his sailing and signalling orders. To avoid attack from the French in the Channel, they took a circuitous route to Europe: up the west coast of Ireland, round the Shetland Isles, down the east coast of Scotland, close to Selkirk's home town, then down the East Coast of England.

Their escort delivered them to the Texel off the northern coast of Holland on 23 July, then sailed on. Danger from the enemy abroad had passed. It seemed they were safely home. The galleon's namesake, John Batchelor, sent his joyful congratulations at 'such wellcome Tydins'.[*]

But still the owners were nervous. There were still threats to their haul. They could not trust the ships' officers and discontented crew. Both their agents, Carleton Vanbrugh and William Bath, had died on the voyage. They sent out a

---

* Batchelor died in November 1711 so never shared in the profits of the galleon named after him.

replacement, James Hollidge, to supervise and report to them. He arrived in Holland on 7 August and wrote that he found Captain Dover well, Captain Courtney 'out of Order wth ye gout', the men mutinous, and 'Capt. Rogers under a great deal of Uneasiness. He seems desperate'.[†]

There was trouble, too, from the London East India Company. Its twenty-four directors were Knights, Aldermen and Whig politicians. They accused the Bristol owners and the privateers of encroaching on their trading charter. They declared themselves 'incensed' at what they perceived as this infringement of their rights. They had the backing of the Bank of England. They aimed to seize the ships, confiscate the prize cargo and arrest the captains. They were doubly provoked by the new Tory administration, which had granted wide trading privileges to its own newly formed South Sea Company. This Company was the idea of the Chancellor of the Exchequer, Sir Robert Harley. His political adviser, Daniel Defoe, in his journal *Review*, championed its aims to the public.[†]

Hollidge took back to London a signed document designed to appease and deter the directors of the East India Company. It said the *Duke* and *Dutchess* had sailed as 'private Men of Warr', that they 'did not traffick in any sort or kind whatsoever', that any cargo sold was only so as 'to furnish themselves with Provisions', that the worm-eaten *Marquess* had been sold 'to buy Necessaries' and that 'not one pin's worth' of cargo had been sold in Amsterdam.

The East India Company directors chose not to believe a word of it. Such protestations were not proof. They sent their own agents to Holland 'to have an eye' on the ships, particularly the *Batchelor*. The crew again threatened mutiny.

There were too many claims to this treasure. Too many owners, agents and toffs with their eyes on it.

At the end of September 1711 a convoy of four naval warships, the *Essex*, *Canterbury*, *Medway* and *Dunwich*, under the command of Rear-Admiral Sir Thomas Hardy, arrived at the Texel to bring back 'ye South Sea men'. There were more delays while Rogers sought permission to refit the treasure galleon. Its sails were rotten and its masts split. He wanted to return in triumph with sails of blue damask and displays of gold. Eyes would be on these ships as they sailed up the Thames. The imminent arrival of the 'Aquapulca Prize' was front-page news in the *Daily Courant*, the *Post-Boy* and the *London Gazette*.[†]

Late on Wednesday 3 October, the ships arrived at the Downs. It was a clear autumn night. Three of the owners were rowed out to welcome and congratulate the men. The *Batchelor* was then towed ahead toward the Thames. It moved up river alone. This was the ship of interest, and Selkirk was its Sailing Master. He wore a swanskin waistcoat, blue linen shirt, new breeches and shoes with scarlet laces. He had been away eight years. He had sailed round the physical world, and for four years and four months survived alone on an uninhabited island. He of all those on this voyage had a story of raw survival, of rags to riches, that men might want to hear.

5

LONDON

SCRIBBLERS

A CRUISING

VOYAGE

ROUND THE

WORLD:

Firſt to the SOUTH-SEAS, thence
to the EAST-INDIES, and homewards
by the Cape of GOOD HOPE.

Begun in 1708, and finiſh'd in 1711.

CONTAINING

A JOURNAL of all the Remarkable
Tranſactions ; particularly, Of the Taking of
Puna and *Guiaquil*, of the *Acapulco* Ship, and
other Prizes ; An Account of *Alexander Selkirk*'s
living alone four Years and four Months in an
Iſland ; and A brief Deſcription of ſeveral Countries in our Courſe noted for Trade, eſpecially
in the *South-Sea*.

With Maps of all the Coaſt, from the beſt *Spaniſh*
Manuſcript Draughts.
And an INTRODUCTION relating to the
SOUTH-SEA Trade.

By Captain *WOODES ROGERS*,
Commander in Chief on this Expedition, with
the Ships *Duke* and *Dutcheſs* of *Briſtol*.

LONDON, Printed for *A. Bell* at the Croſs-Keys and Bible
in *Cornhil*, and *B. Lintot* at the Croſs-Keys between the
two Temple-Gates, *Fleetſtreet*. M DCC. XII.

The Most Barren Subject that Nature Can Afford　　1712

WOODES ROGERS and Edward Cooke had both kept journals of their quest for the Manila treasure ship. Back in London they hurried to outsmart each other in book form. There was a readership for first-hand accounts of plundering voyages, to exotic far-off places across dangerous seas. It was fashionable 'to go round the globe with Dampier' as Daniel Defoe put it.

Neither Rogers nor Cooke had Dampier's skill for travel writing, his range, or flair for anecdote. Beyond shipboard life, their observations were more of the 'winds south, south-east, anchored at Guam' sort. But Dampier had no book to offer of this voyage. His days of fame were gone. He was given no praise for the Acapulco haul. Comment on him by fellow mariners was scathing. While he was away, William Funnell had published his own scornful account of the previous failed voyage.[†] Dampier became caught in renewed blame and litigation and his waning energy was used in trying to vindicate his reputation and clear his name.[†]

Edward Cooke feared that more notice would be taken of

Woodes Rogers' book than his own. Rogers had been Commander in Chief of the whole expedition and had eminent
literary friends. At Bartram's Coffee House in Church Street,
opposite Hungerford Market in the Strand, he met with
Richard Steele, pamphleteer, playwright, essayist and author
of the daily paper the *Spectator* and with the equally prolific
Daniel Defoe who wrote and published the *Review*.

Cooke had for a short time been captain of the worm-eaten
prize the *Marquess*, sold at Batavia, for scrap. He had no influ-
ential friends. To get ahead of Rogers, he brought out his
book in two parts. The first volume was on sale by March
1712, four months after the ships were home. He called it
*A Voyage to the South Sea and Round the World Perform'd in
the Years 1708, 1709, 1710 and 1711 by the Ships* Duke *and*
Dutchess *of Bristol*.

To imply high patronage he dedicated it to Sir Robert
Harley. On the title page he was advised by his publisher to
advertise 'an Account of Mr Alexander Selkirk, his Manner
of living and taming some wild Beasts during the four Years
and four Months he liv'd upon the uninhabited Island of Juan
Fernandes'.

But the 'Account' Cooke gave his readers was confined to
one meagre paragraph. Selkirk, he told them, had been Master
of the *Cinque Ports Galley*. He had had some unspecified disagreement with his captain and 'the ship being leaky he had
gone ashore'. He had survived on goat meat, cabbages that
grow on trees, on turnips and parsnips. He tamed wild goats
and cats. When rescued, he was wearing a goatskin jacket,
breeches and cap, all 'sewed with thongs of the same'. And
that was the sum of it. What more was there to say? Cooke

turned his attention to storms, gunboats, plunder, and disputes among the crew.

Readers felt cheated. This story of abandonment whetted curiosity. They wanted more of it. Who was Selkirk? What had he felt? How, in detail, had he survived?

Cooke was encouraged by his publisher to fill the gap with his second volume. In an irascible preface to it he promised 'a fuller Account of the Man found on the Island'. He complained he had been rushed into print for the first part of his book with insufficient time to research details.

That short Hint rais'd the Curiosity of some Persons to expect a more particular Relation of the Man's manner of living in that tedious Solitude. We are naturally fond of Novelty and this Propension inclines us to look for something very extraordinary in any Accident that happens out of the common Course. To hear of a Man's living so long alone in a desert Island, seems to some very surprizing and they presently conclude he may afford a very agreeable Relation of his Life when in Reality it is the most barren Subject that Nature can afford.

Cooke met with Selkirk and questioned him, but saw no scope to his story. It was, in his view, dull and inconsequential to be interminably alone, without company or comfort, on a bit of land he described as an 'entire Heap of Rocks', so steep as to look 'almost perpendicular'. He was not, he wrote, going to pander to romanticism or invent. The discerning reader would, he felt sure, want truth not fiction. Not many people wanted to read about 'ancient Authorities', in the Egyptian desert, who eked out solitary lives of austerity and devotion.

What then can it be that flatters our Curiosity? Is Selkirk a natural Philosopher, who, by such an undisturb'd Retirement could make any surprizing Discoveries? Nothing less, we have a downright Sailor, whose only Study was how to support himself, during his Confinement and all his Conversation with Goats.

So Cooke gave again the bones of Selkirk's adventure. The frigates of the *Duke* and *Dutchess* had sailed into the Great Bay of The Island. Their crew saw a man waving a white flag. They called to him to show them a good place to land. He gave directions, then 'ran along the Shore in Sight of the Boat so swiftly that the native Goats could not have outstripp'd him'. When invited to the ship, 'he first enquir'd whether a certain Officer he knew was Aboard'. If so, he would remain in solitude, rather than sail with him.

He had an axe and other tools, a pot to boil meat. He had made a spit and a bedstead and 'tam'd a Parcel of Goats'. He 'knew all the by Ways and Paths on the Mountains, could trip from one Crag to another, and let himself down the dreadful Precipices'. He had kept an exact account of the day of the month and the week. He had taken Captain Frye into the mountains to 'a pleasant spot full of Grass and furnish'd with Trees' where he had built his lodging place and a kitchen.

His greatest disaster was when he fell down a precipice and lay for dead. Somehow he crawled to his hut and survived. He survived, too, when Spaniards landed on The Island, by hiding from them. They pursued him but he was to them 'a Prize being so inconsiderable, it is likely they thought it not worth while to be at any great Trouble to find it'.

Cooke supposed the Spaniards were as uninterested as he was in Selkirk. There was no cause for wonder in this story, no pause for thought. A man marooned was another happening. It merited no more than a paragraph or two. It was hard to spin it out. It was an incident of personal misfortune, irrelevant to the true purpose of the voyage, an 'Accident out of the Common Cause', no more significant than Icarus falling from the sky.

A Plain and Temperate Way of Living   1712

WOODES ROGERS needed his book to be a commercial success.[†] His unease and desperation were not mitigated by his return to England. Half his face had been shot away, he walked with a limp, he was accused of embezzlement and his share of the treasure was contested. At home in Bristol he had debts which he could not pay. His father-in-law, Admiral Whetstone, was dead, his wife had cooled towards him and he had three children to maintain. To escape his creditors, he declared himself bankrupt.

He was a man of no particular education, his journal entries were circumstantial, and he wanted literary polish to his seaman's prose. It would not, he knew, woo readers to tell them, as did Cooke, that Selkirk's story was 'the most barren Subject that Nature can afford'.

He sought Richard Steele's help. Steele was a fat man, fond of drink and prone to gout. He walked with a cane and on bad days with crutches.* He could not have chased goats on an uninhabited island, or survived scrimp rations in a leaky ship. But he saw in Selkirk's story evidence of Christian piety, the vanity of riches and the indomitability of Man.

He was curious to meet this abandoned man. Rogers

---

*Woodes Rogers introduced Steele to women who, he said, would make him 'throw away his cane and dance a minuet'. To one of these, a Mrs Roach, Steele paid some hundreds of pounds.

introduced them and they had Coffee House conversations at the end of 1711. Steele questioned Selkirk in line with his own interest: what had been his quarrel with Stradling, what possessions did he have when marooned, what creatures threatened him, what did he eat, how did he endure the isolation, what sort of dwelling had he built, what did he read, how often did he pray, how did he cope with his return to society, how had the experience of The Island changed him.

Rogers called his book *A Cruising Voyage Round the World*. To vie with Cooke his title page advertised 'the Taking of the Acapulco Ship and An Account of Alexander Selkirk living alone four Years and four Months in an Island'. His version was more than a tale of derring-do, fortune hunting and of a marooned man who survived to make the journey home. Selkirk was transmuted into a Christian, a Patriot, the Governor of The Island.

Rogers gave again the facts of abandonment, the possessions Selkirk had, the huts he built, the clothes he sewed. But in the minds of those who could not know The Island, its seisms, eruptions and squalling winds, its ravines and jagged peaks, its yellow orchids, spiny bromeliae and hummingbirds, Selkirk had been alone four years and months on an indeterminate bit of land – sand, with scant palms and an encircling sea. It was not The Island that was of interest, it was Man, who in the image of God, got the better of wherever he was. 'Nothing but the Divine Providence' Rogers was prompted to write, 'could have supported any Man.'

Selkirk, in his isolation, moved from piracy to piety, from rape and plunder to a state of grace. Abandoned on The Island he did not fuck goats or rail at the sky. 'He employ'd himself in reading, singing Psalms and praying.'

Solitude and Retirement from the World is not such an unsufferable State of Life as most Men imagine, especially when People are fairly call'd or thrown into it unavoidably, as this Man was.

Selkirk was sustained not by The Island but by God. In his closeness to God he 'found means to supply his Wants in a very natural manner'. Scavenging for food and chopping trees for shelter was inconvenient, but the results were on a par with 'all our Arts and Society'. And there was a moral for readers, comfortable in their libraries and lounges:

how much a plain and temperate way of living conduces to the Health of the Body and the Vigour of the Mind, both of which we are apt to destroy by Excess and Plenty, especially of strong Liquor, and the Variety as well as the Nature of our Meat and Drink: for this Man when he came to our ordinary Method of Diet and Life, tho he was sober enough, lost much of his Strength and Agility. But I must quit these Reflections, which are more proper for a Philosopher and Divine than a Mariner.

Selkirk read this account of who he was and concurred. Perhaps it was like that. God determined the day. Time had passed. The experience was distanced. Memories were lost and fragmented. It was all over in a temporal way, the extravagant isolation, the ordeal of life without a human voice. On The Island waves broke loud against the ridge of the shore.

When I Was Not Worth a Farthing   1713

ONE YEAR later, Richard Steele profited on his own account from Selkirk's adventure. Like Rogers, Steele was in debt and acquainted with creditors.[†] He faced repeated lawsuits for money. He owed to his tailor, goldsmith and upholsterer and for arrears in rent, and to friends. Even Joseph Addison, a literary collaborator since their schooldays, went to court to recover money from him.*Steele needed to make his pen pay.

In October 1713 he started a journal, the *Englishman*.** His intention with it was 'to rouze in this divided Nation that lost Thing called Publick Spirit'. He published it until February 1714. He said that it exposed him 'to much Hatred and Invective'. His 'Brother Scribbler' Jonathan Swift was rude about it and him:

Mr Steele publishes every day a penny paper, to be read in coffee-houses and get him a little money... He hath no invention, nor is master of a tolerable style... Being the most imprudent man alive, he never follows the advice of his friends, but is wholly at the mercy of fools or knaves, or hurried away by his own caprice; by which he hath committed more absurdities in economy, friendship, love, duty, good manners, politics, religion and writing, than ever fell to one man's share.†

In the *Englishman* Steele wrote about Patriotism, Passive Obedience and the Protestant Succession. Occasionally he diverted to lighter things. Issue 21 was on the pleasures of a country drive in a chaise, 34 was about a visit to Oxford, and 26 was devoted to Selkirk on The Island.

With a journalist's flam, at the start of this article Steele promised to relate 'an Adventure so uncommon, that it's doubtful whether the like has happen'd to any of human Race'. To give a sense of verity he told of the conversations

---

*Addison and Steele when students shared lodgings in Bury Street. They co-wrote the *Tatler*. Addison was godfather to Steele's eldest daughter, Elizabeth. In 1711 Steele owed Addison £100.

**On 1 October 1713 the last issue, no. 175, of the *Guardian* appeared. On 6 October, the first number of the *Englishman, Being the Sequel to the Guardian,* was published.

he had held with Selkirk in 1711. From Selkirk's demeanour Steele claimed to discern that 'he had been much separated from Company'. Selkirk, he wrote, had 'a strong but chearful Seriousness in his Look, and a certain Disregard to the ordinary things about him, as if he had been sunk in Thought.'*

Solitude on Juan Fernandez had been sheer romance. The Island Steele would never glimpse was 'the most delicious Bower, fann'd with continual Breezes and gentle Aspirations of Wind'. Selkirk's 'Repose after the Chase' in the hut he had made, was 'equal to the most sensual Pleasures' of town life.

He never had a Moment heavy upon his Hands; his Nights were untroubled, and his Days joyous, from the Practice of Temperance and Exercise.

Abandonment enriched him. From it, he learned the value of simplicity. He listened to barking seals with pleasure and danced with goats and kittens. Return to the World, Steele said, with all its joys, could not compensate Selkirk for his loss. And there was a moral to this adventure for readers of the *Englishman* to observe:

This plain Man's Story is a memorable Example, that he is happiest who confines his Wants to natural Necessities; and he that goes further in his Desires, increases his Wants in Proportion to his Acquisitions; or to use his own Expression, *I am now worth 800 Pounds, but shall never be so happy, as when I was not worth a Farthing.*

The virtue of poverty was a Christian ideal often not espoused by its advocates. Steele did not confine his Wants to natural Necessities. He had a family house at Hampton Wick

---

*Between 1709 and 1711, Selkirk had not had a moment's separation from Company. He had been off The Island for three years.

and a chariot with four horses. He employed Richard the foot-man, a gardener, a boy called Will, a woman called Watts, and a boy who spoke Welsh. He liked his coffee hot, his arm-chairs deep and his wines of the vintage sort.

Some months after their conversations together in 1711, Selkirk met Steele by chance in the street. He greeted him expecting an exchange of conversation. Steele could not recollect having seen him before. He had to be reminded who Selkirk was. He had remembered the story, but not the man.

1712 *Gold Ingots and 2 Casks of Decay'd Tea Bisquetts*

SELKIRK HAD a battle to get his share of the plunder – the eight hundred pounds derided by Steele. On its arrival in London, the cargo from the treasure galleon was swarmed over by owners and officers, officials and lawyers. There were accusations of embezzlement, cheating and lies.

He had hoped to go to Largo to visit his family. But he would not leave London until the auctions were over and the courts had ruled on who should get what. If he left town, or signed on for another voyage, he feared he would get nothing.

Storing and sorting the cargo began on 11 December 1712 under the supervision of Robert Patterson. His bill came to £311 10s for 623 days work at 10 shillings a day. It was one of a plethora of expenses, all extravagantly deducted. There were charges for making boxes and barrels, bagging raw and thrown silk, for sorting lace, boxing pepper, renting warehouses and sale rooms, for printing and advertising, for packers' fees, for coffees and teas at Wills Coffee House and wine at the Dolphin Tavern.

The waterman who guided the ships up the Thames put in a bill for £34 16s. Mr Montague wanted £107 10s for sorting silk. £300 went in 'tavern expenses and treats'. Henry Coleman charged £54 8s for clothes for Negro slaves so that they might look respectable at the point of sale. Samuel Smith fitted them with shoes for £3 15s.

There were eight auctions of plunder 'by the candle' in 1712 and 1713 at the Marine Coffee House in Cornhill and at Edmund Crisp's Coffee House. Bids were received for as long as a small piece of candle burned. The last bid before the candle went out secured each lot.

Gold ingots, pieces of eight and pearls fetched four thousand pounds. But much of the valuable stuff had disappeared. Members of the crew reiterated that Woodes Rogers had hidden away treasure at Batavia so that he might secretly collect it later.

Merchants from all over the country gathered for these auctions. They bid for china, bales of silk, silk stockings, linens, towels, calicos, spices, cast iron, beeswax, ribbons and taffetas, a chest of priests' vestments, six dozen handbells, twenty-four pictures painted on copper in oils, a 'great bewgle', cocoa, yarn, flowered muslin, chintzes, quilts, shirts, smocks, drawers, petticoats and forty-five counterpanes stitched with silk.*

The total raised for the plunder was £147,975 12s 4d, a sum far below the expectation of the men. The Lord Chancellor ruled that two thirds of this should go to the owners, and one

*These inventories and accounts, muddled and unsorted, are in dusty boxes in Chancery C104/36, in the Public Record Office, London. And see David J. Starkey, *British Privateering Enterprise in the Eighteenth Century* (1990).

third to the crew, according to the original terms of agreement. But before any payments were made the Chancery Courts had to judge and rule on the depositions, submissions, grievances and pleas that came from all involved.

Bribes were paid. The East India Company, persistent in their accusation that their trading rights had been infringed, was bought off for £6000 plus £161 5s to an unnamed official.[†] Payment was also made to The Company of Silk Throwers, who controlled the import of silk from Persia, China and the East Indies. One hundred and forty-nine pounds went in bribes to Custom House Officers.

Predictably the crew fared worst. Three years went by before they got anything. They claimed they should receive £1000 a share, not the £42 6s eventually authorised by the Master in Chancery. In signed petitions they accused the owners and ships' officers of 'vile and clandestine practices' such as destroying the Bills of Lading, of selling off prize vessels and of sending home silver plate in East India Company ships.

It was, the crewmen said, by the 'Courage and Hazzard of their lives' that the treasure galleon had been taken. Seventy of them had died on the voyage. Those that survived, and their families, were 'perishing from Want of Bread and daily thrown into Gaols', while all their complaints were pushed aside.

Selkirk did well to get his two and a half share. He got eight hundred pounds, four gold rings, a silver tobacco box, a gold-headed cane, a pair of gold candlesticks and a silver-hilted sword. From this had been deducted what he owed for sewing silk, serge, a jacket and tobacco. He fared better than

Christopher Dewars who was among those who had died. His mother collected the £3 8s 6d deemed due, and left her thumb print by way of receipt. Men forced by time to move on or away, received not a penny for their courage, or the hazard of their lives. They had, said their lawyer, been 'blinded and kept in the Dark, nay Defrauded in a clandestine and unfair manner.'

All Things in Hugger Mugger   1712

AMONG THOSE wanting a cut of the Acapulco booty were the heirs of Thomas Estcourt. It rankled with them that Dampier stood to gain from this haul. They still smarted over the loss of their money in the fiasco of his 1703 voyage and held him responsible for the sinking of both their ships and the waste of all their investment.

He had gone to sea again in 1708 without the conclusion of their legal case against him and they intended to relieve him of such funds as he had, or that might be owing to him. He was fifty-eight and ill and was unlikely to disappear on another voyage.

Estcourt's younger sister and heir, Elizabeth Cresswell and her husband, prepared their case against him. Their charge was that he mismanaged the 1703 voyage, concealed plunder taken, and used embezzled money from the first voyage to finance the second. They paid Selkirk to give witness against him.

Selkirk was compliant in telling people whatever they wanted to hear, if it was to his advantage. He gave evidence to the Cresswells' agent on 18 July 1712, in the form of a signed

Deposition.[†] He was lodging with a Thomas Ronquillo, at a house near St Catherine's in the County of Middlesex. He had found a woman whom he described as a 'loveing friend', Katherine Mason. She had a husband, John, who was a merchant tailor.

Selkirk gave his age as thirty-two, and described himself as a Mariner. He was, he said, 'in a short time going on a long voyage to some remote Isles beyond the Seas.' He did not explain the island of his destination. Perhaps it was The Island of his abandonment, The Island that he knew.

His evidence damned Dampier. The *Cinque Ports* and the *St George* were, he said, good ships, worth together about £6000. They sank because they had not been sheathed:

and it must needs be a great fault in the Deft Dampier not to advise that they be sheathed ... having been Severall Voyages to the South Seas before the voyage above mentioned he must needs know that the worms there eat Ships for the worms there doe eat Shipps extreamly bad & as bad as in any other pt of the World & the not sheathing the Ships St George & Cinque Ports Galley was the loss of both ships for they Perished by being worm Eaten.

Selkirk's picture of the 1703 voyage was of mismanagement, deception, incompetence, cowardice and greed. He said, or was prompted to say, that all Articles of Agreement between officers and crew had been broken. No entries of plunder were ever recorded or accounts kept. 'Dampier, Morgan & Stradling took upon themselves without consulting others to manage & Do what they pleased.' They stole money and silver plate, 'managed all things in hugger mugger among themselves', and paid out no dividends to the crew.

Selkirk described how Dampier callously marooned his First Lieutenant James Barnaby. He said the French ship, sighted at the end of February 1704, from The Island, was worth £12,000, and if the men had been allowed to fight it, they would have taken it. It was Dampier who denied them the opportunity, saying 'he knew how to make advantage of the Voyage otherwise'.

In March and April 1704, Selkirk said, they had taken five or six Spanish ships as prizes. He put their total value at £50,000. In one were 'Divers Chests of Silver to the value of £20,000'. Dampier's refusal to let the men rummage this ship for plunder, caused the break-up of the voyage.

Other witnesses, Ralph Clift and William Sheltram, corroborated Selkirk's allegations.[†] Clift admitted that he himself was illiterate. None the less he confirmed that no records were kept of the voyage, nor council meetings held. Dampier, he said, went against the advice of the owners in not having the ships sheathed, 'telling them there were no worms where they were going'. He 'behaved himself the whole voyage very ill & very rudely & very vilely both to his officers & Men'. He and Morgan 'took Ingots or Wedges both of silver & also of Gold'. These were worth at least £10,000, and they sold them at Batavia. It was Dampier's 'fault and mismanagement' and his threatening to shoot the Steersman through the head, that lost the 'Acapulca Ship' and lost the Owners 'two Millions of money'.

Sheltram concurred. It was Dampier's fault that the 'Acopulca ship' got away.[*] He 'refused to be ruled' or to follow advice. The St George was 'like a Ceive She was eaten by worms soe much'. Men had to 'Pump Day & Night to gett the

---

*There was no agreement by any scribe about the spelling of Acapulco.

water out of her'. Dampier 'did behave himself very indecently, abusing both the Officers and Men & giving them very base and abusive Language'. He and Morgan 'took a very considerable Quantity of Pearle and two Bales of wrought silk' and hid it all away at Batavia and Amsterdam. All he, Sheltram, ever received were ten Pieces of Eight.

The Cresswells' case against Dampier was not heard before a judge. The mariners' allegations could not be proved. Words might have been put into their mouths. Dampier was sick and clearly not rich. In a will dated 1714, he described himself as 'diseased and weak in body, but of sound and perfect mind'. He died the following year aged sixty-one leaving debts of around two thousand pounds.

1712 *The South Sea Bubble*

THERE WAS always another journey to make, other prizes to be won. It seemed that Selkirk's long voyage to remote Isles, beyond the Seas, was to be with the new South Sea Company. Peace between England and Spain was imminent in 1712 and English exclusion from the South Sea would end. A huge expeditionary force was planned to set up trading posts along the coast of South America. It would sail in June. 'There has not been in our Memory an Undertaking of such Consequence' Defoe wrote in an *Essay on the South-Sea Trade*.[†]

We shall, under the Protection, in the Name, and by the Power of Her Majesty, Seize, Take and Possess such Port or Place, or Places, Land, Territory, Country or Dominion, *call it what you please*, as we see fit in *America*, and *Keep it for our own*. Keeping it implies Planting, Settling, Inhabiting, Spreading, and all that is usual in such Cases: And *when this is done*, what are we to do with it? Why, we are to Trade *to* it, and *from* it; *Whither?* Where ever we can with Spaniards, or any Body that will Trade with us.

The Company's objectives were, he said, 'capable of being the Greatest, most Valuable, most Profitable, and most Encreasing Branch of Trade in our whole British Commerce.' Its profits would pay off the national debt – which stood at nine million pounds, lead to trading agreements with Spain and bring wealth to all involved.[†]

The expeditionary fleet of 1712, would have 20 warships and bomb vessels, 40 transport ships, hospital ships and 4000 soldiers. Woodes Rogers was to command it. He met at South Sea House with the deputy governor of the South Sea Company, Sir James Bateman.

Selkirk would go too. His Island would be colonised. He knew its virtues. It was safe for ships. It would bring great riches to Great Britain. It had given to him, it would give to others too. He would advise on its harbours and tides, its topography and climate, where to build and when to plant.

The Company spent £120,000 on fitting ships, but more investment was needed. In March, the Secretary of State, Henry St John, pledged government money for this voyage 'to carry on the Trade to those Parts'.[†] Queen Anne intimated that she would 'be pleased to assist this Company with a Sufficient Force'.

Selkirk hung around the port of Bristol drinking flip in the bars. Month after month went by. No money for the grand scheme came. The Treaty of Utrecht was signed. It marked peace with Spain and gave trading rights to the South Sea Company. But letters from the Company to the Most Honourable Robert, Earl of Oxford, Lord High Treasurer of

Great Britain and to Queen Anne went unanswered.

Selkirk waited. He believed this voyage must happen. It seemed inconceivable that such grand plans should come to nothing and such effort and money be squandered. He wanted again to sail with Rogers, the man who had rescued him, who called him Governor and Monarch. He wanted again to see The Island.

The safe time for sailing passed. The acquired ships stayed idle. Their cargoes rotted. The South Sea scheme was a shining bubble, floating high and filled with air. The Island, remote and far beyond the seas, receded. Selkirk would not return to it. Boredom and drink led to trouble. On 23 September 1713 he was charged in the parish of St Stephens in Bristol, with common assault. He had beaten up Richard Nettle, a sailor. As with previous brushes with the law he did not show up for the hearing.[†] He moved to the obscurity of London for some months, then went home to Largo.

6

HOME

Alexander Selkirk: Marrinir aged 32 years or thereab.ts lodged Thomas Rowquhols house near St Katherins in the County of Midd.x Sworne of Faith

That this Dep. sayled the voyage now in quion on board the ship Cinq Ports Gally as Mar of her ... then when she went out of the River of ... a good new ship in very good condition as to body ... sayled ... stored & all other ... & was very well fitted out in all things ...

Selkirk's Deposition of 1712 and the house where he was born.

Punch or Flip 1714

EIGHT HUNDRED POUNDS would buy the streets of Largo.
The family legend was that Selkirk returned to his home town
on a Sunday morning in Spring in gold-laced clothes. There
was no one at his father's house. He went to the Church. His
parents were there. His mother, 'uttering a cry of joy',

Even in the house of God, rushed to his arms, unconscious of the im-
propriety of her conduct and the interruption of the service.[†]

He had booty to show for his danger and daring. He
impressed them with 'Several Summes of Money', silver and
gold, 'a considerable Parcell of Linnen Cloth', his sea books
and instruments, the accounts of his adventures by Edward
Cooke, Woodes Rogers and Richard Steele.

He had with him, too, his glazed, brown stoneware flip-can
and four years and four months of The Island etched into his

mind. Drink was again an addiction, a kind of rescue. The can was engraved with a rhyme:

> Alexander Selkirk, this is my One
> When you me take on Board of Ship
> Pray fill me full with Punch or Flip[†]

Largo had stayed still. The wide bay, grey ocean and low sky, the houses huddled by the harbour, the little fishing boats. There were the same habits of survival. The slaughter of farm animals, the drying of their hides, the harvesting of crops, the same prayers on Sundays, declaring gratitude, asking for forgiveness, profit and everlasting life.

His mother, Euphan, was ill. His brother, David, now ran the tannery. He had a son named Alexander. Selkirk lodged first with his parents, then with his brother John and sister-in-law Margaret. But he was more estranged than ever from family life. He could not cope with its confinement and circumspection, the small-time conversation, the meals at table. He took no part in the daily round, was taciturn and at times in tears.

There was a rocky piece of land, high and fissured with rocks behind his father's house. Here he built a kind of cave. His consolation in the day was to be there alone and watch the sea. He watched perhaps for a passing sail. 'O my beloved Island!' he was supposed to have said. 'I wish I had never left thee.'

He tried to create the civilised life he had imagined on The Island. He bought a large house by the Craigie Well in Largo. He acquired adjacent 'Lands, Tenements, Outhouses, Gardens, Yards and Orchards'. He found a naïve and compliant woman Sophia Bruce, the daughter of a crofter, whom he thought might be his wife. Her parents were dead and she survived on the charity of three uncles, all ministers: 'Mr Harry Rymer, Mr James Rymer and another'.[†]

Selkirk liked to meet her secretly high in the woodland of Keil's Den, or in the ruins of Pitcruvie Castle among the ferns, grasses and bluebells. She endured his drinking, his moods and violence, was moved by his story and impressed by his wealth. She pitied his abandonment for all those years in an unimaginable place. He supposed he would marry her though she was no more to him than The Island's goats, the women of Guayaquil, or Loathsome Negroes from a stolen prize. He called her his 'beloved friend', but the swamps of Darien, the ferocious winds of the southern ocean, the taunts and jeers of shipboard life, scavenging for sustenance alone on an island… none of it had primed him to be a married man.

The sea was more real than a woman, the force of the tides. The Island resonated. He bought a boat and sailed the bay to the cliffs of Kingscraig Point. He lingered where the sea and land elided, observed the straddle of seaweed, the calling birds.

He left Largo in a hurry, never to return. After a drinking bout he beat a young man almost to death.[†] The young man's life was despaired of. Yet again, Selkirk did not face the inquiry that followed. He abandoned his attempts at status, the house and land he had bought. He took with him his plunder and money and Sophia Bruce. He left his sea chest, clothes and flip-can.

1717 *She Said He Married Her*

HE RENTED a house in Pall Mall and was sheltered again by the streets of London. The adventures of the past receded. Dampier was dead, Woodes Rogers had been appointed Governor of the Bahamas and was ridding the area of 'loose people and pirates'.[†] Selkirk sought a more ordinary life. Sophia Bruce asked for marriage, and he agreed.

The sea lured so he enlisted in the Navy. He joined HMS *Enterprise* as Mate. It was an unremarkable job. The *Enterprise* was a merchant ship that plied the Channel ports taking and unloading cargo. Its destiny was not remote and far-off Isles beyond the Seas. There were no pirates or prizes, no storms or volcanoes, no chasing of goats or hiding in trees.[†]

While the ship was being fitted, he made a Will. He signed it in Wapping on 13 January 1717. It 'Called to Mind the Perills and Dangers of the Seas and other uncertaintys of this transitory life'. Sophia Bruce was its main beneficiary and his executor. In it, he left ten pounds to Katherine Mason who had consoled him when he first reached London. His father who was ill and old was, while he lived, to have the Largo house. Then it was to go to Sophia. She was to manage it, levy rents, and profit from it 'to all intents as I myself might or could do being personally present'. After her death it was to pass to his nephew Alexander.[†]

All his disposable wealth was for his 'Loveing Friend', Sophia: his lands, gardens and orchards, his wages, money, gold, silver, clothes, his 'Linnen and Woolin', everything owed to him as a mariner, 'tickets, pensions, prize money, smart money, legacies and dues'.

She said he married her. She gave the wedding day as 4 March 1717 but was vague as to where the ceremony took place or who witnessed it. Perhaps a notary took a fee and gave or did not give some salient piece of paper. Woodes Rogers had observed how, at Kinsale, men were 'continually marrying'. They soon parted for all time from their brides.

Selkirk was away at sea eight months. When he returned he and Sophia resumed a kind of married life for nine months more. He was taciturn and absent. He drank too much, was violent and unsettled, but she thought she had the status of his wife, the security of inheritance, some sort of commitment from him. When the *Enterprise* left again, and he with it, she took it as part of the bargain of being a mariner's wife: to be together then apart, alone then reunited. She had reason to believe him. He had bound his intentions in the language of the law. It was written down that she was his 'trusty and love-ing friend', his 'full and sole executrix'. Were he to die, he had recommended his soul into the hands of Almighty God, asked for his body to be committed to the earth or sea, and promised all his worldly goods to her.

The Life and Strange Surprizing Adventures   1719
of Robinson Crusoe

SO SELKIRK became a naval officer, on a wage, with a pen-sion and familial obligations. His story of abandonment faded, like the news of a day. He had survived alone on an unaccommodating island when all human support was with-drawn. He had made this island his home. But rescue meant return to society. And now he was with HMS *Enterprise*, plying the unremarkable ports of Sheerness and Woolwich, Plymouth and Portsmouth.

While he was employed on this ordinary voyage, Daniel Defoe picked up the tale again. Selkirk's 'Fame of having lived four Years and four Months alone in the island of *Juan Fernandez*' inspired Defoe to write a novel. He called it 'The Life and Strange Surprizing Adventures of Robinson Crusoe, of York, mariner: Who lived Eight and Twenty Years, all alone in an uninhabited Island on the Coast of America, near the Mouth of the Great River of Oronoque; Having been cast on Shore by Shipwreck, wherein all the Men perished but himself. An account of how he was at last as strangely deliver'd by Pyrates'.*

It was the first English novel and became known as *Robinson Crusoe*. Defoe was nearing sixty when he wrote it. He lived in a 'very genteel' manner, in a house in Stoke Newington. He had a fine library, stables, a large garden and seven children.

Like Steele he was in debt and keen for money. He needed cash to pay for his daughter Maria's wedding.** *Robinson Crusoe* took him a few months to write and was his four hundred and twelfth publication.*** He did not wrestle with his prose. He was the author of daily broadsheets, political and religious essays, satires in verse, odes and hymns. He propounded tolerance, reason and practical work, advocated free trade, union between Scotland and England, the establishment of savings banks, and a review of bankruptcy laws. He denounced

*Oronoque was a fictional river.
**Maria Defoe married a salter, a Mr Langley.
***Defoe defeats bibliography. He probably wrote some 560 books, pamphlets and journals. Sixteen were published in 1719, the same year as *Robinson Crusoe*.

corruption at elections, and the persecution of dissenters.*

Fiction, though, was new ground. He intended *Robinson Crusoe* as a money-making yarn. It was published anonymously on 25 April 1719, reprinted on 9 May, 4 June and 7 August and from then on. There was no definitive manuscript. The first edition was changed even while at the printers.†

The book was a winner. Here was the quintessential survival story: a man cut off from the world, who trusted in God and did what he could for himself. Though Defoe was chided for 'Solecisms, Looseness and Incorrectness of Stile, Improbabilities, and sometimes Impossibilities', his readers were undeterred.** They identified, projected and asked the question, what would I do, if that were to happen to me?

Robinson Crusoe was serialised, abridged, pirated, adapted, dramatised and bowdlerised. It was translated into French in 1720 and into Dutch, German and Russian in the 1760s. It was banned in Spain in 1756. An abridged French version of 1769, gave Richard Steele as the author. In the 1770s it was printed as a Chapbook, a penny book printed on a single sheet of paper, folded twelve times, and distributed by walking stationers called chapmen, hired by printers, who sold it in towns on market days.

It became a world classic. By 1863 it was in the Shilling

The Shortest Way with the Dissenters, 1703, satirised extreme Tory views and provoked official wrath. Threatened with prison, Defoe went into hiding in Spitalfields. An informant who flushed him out got a reward of £50. Defoe was pilloried on three consecutive days, then sent to Newgate gaol. His satire was publicly burned.

**Among the anomalies in the first edition, Crusoe's wrecked ship was carried out of sight by the storm, but was visible a few pages later. He stripped off his clothes to swim to the wreck, then filled his pockets with biscuits from it.

Entertaining Library, by 1869 there was 'Robinson Crusoe in words of one syllable' by Mary Godolphin, with coloured illustrations, and by 1900 it was being given away in promotions by grocers. Crusoe inspired literary criticism, picture books, pop-up books, cartoons, puppets and pantomimes. His image was universal. He was portrayed standing alone on a circle of sand, with a palm tree and the surrounding sea; barefoot in goat skins with a musket at his shoulder and a sinking ship behind him; leaning on a rock with a spy glass and umbrella; shooting goats, discovering Man Friday's footprint in the sand.*

Down the years, Selkirk transmuted into Crusoe's mythical world. His own reality blurred. His time on The Island, claimed first by journalists, was reinvented in the bright world of fiction. What had really happened and who he was were incidental. It was the story that mattered, not The Island or the man.

Defoe capitalised on *Crusoe*'s success. Within a year he produced two sequels: *The Farther Adventures of Robinson Crusoe; Being the Second and Last Part of His Life and of the Strange Surprizing Accounts of his Travels Round three Parts of the Globe*, and then, in 1720, a work of awful piety, *Serious Reflections During the Life and Surprizing Adventures of Robinson Crusoe: With his Vision of the Angelic World*. In a preface to this he teased:

there is a man alive, and well known too, the actions of whose life are the

---

*The quantity of scholarship about *Robinson Crusoe* is truly extraordinary. A *Concordance* (1998), more than a thousand pages long, lists the number of times Defoe uses words in the book: Providence (55 times), Island (183), Time (294), Earthquake (8).

just subject of these volumes, and to whom all or most part of the story most directly alludes.

Part Two was widely published if not widely read. Part Three was instantly forgotten. And of the thousands of references and allusions to Robinson Crusoe that were to follow, none were to Crusoe in China, Russia, France, Persia, India, Russia, or Heaven. They were all to the core theme: the Man alone on the island.

A Large Earthenware Pot   1719

CRUSOE'S ISLAND was an unexplained place, though he inhabited it alone for twenty-eight years. He was swept to its shore by a storm that wrecked his ship and all those on it except himself. The sea that saved him and drowned them was 'as high as a great hill, and as furious as an enemy'. It buried him under thirty-foot waves.

His island, like Selkirk's, was volcanic, part of an archipelago and uninhabited by man. It was susceptible to earthquake, with freak waves and hurricanes, great rains and uprooted trees. It had mountains and a brook of running water. But it had scant reality of its own. It existed to serve Crusoe. Providence dictated that it should be his estate. It 'looked like a planted garden'. 'Leadenhall Market could not have furnished a better table.' It provided him with pigeons, hares, lobsters, tobacco, sugar, melons, grapes, cocoa, oranges, lemons and limes.

But more than this unmysterious market garden, his true storehouse was the wreck of the ship from which he escaped. From it, he retrieved all he needed for civilised life. Its contents rivalled that of a fleet of prize ships. It was astonishing what was spared by the sea as high as a hill and as furious as an enemy.

He made a raft and salvaged supplies for more than a lifetime: gallons of liquor (enough for twenty-eight years), chests of bread, rice, cheeses, dried meat and corn, barrels of tobacco, flour and sugar, cables, hawsers, carpentry tools, barrels of gunpowder, quantities of ammunition, pistols, swords, two dozen hatchets, a grindstone, crowbars, bags of nails, clothes, hammocks, bedding, sails, rigging, canvas, ironwork, scissors, knives, forks, pens, ink, paper, compasses, mathematical instruments, charts, books on navigation, a 'perspective glass', three bibles and some Portuguese prayer books.

Thus supplied, he insulated himself against his fictional island. He was gentrified, with a 'country seat', a bower, kitchen, orchard and winter stores. He was 'removed from all the wickedness of the world... the lust of the flesh, the lust of the eye, the pride of life'. No goat fucking for Crusoe. Like Selkirk he went barefoot, but unlike Selkirk he had scissors with which to cut his hair and beard, and shape his moustache into 'Mahometan whiskers'.

He ate raisins for breakfast, broiled goat for lunch and turtles' eggs for supper. He built huts and a barn for his corn. He made tables and chairs, hollowed a canoe, made an umbrella, wove 'an abundance of necessary baskets', tailored breeches and waistcoats and fashioned a hat. He made a goatskin belt to carry his hatchet, saw and guns, and he made very good candles out of goats' tallow. He caged a parrot and called it Poll; it spoke his name.

No man could have applied himself more. His production

was extraordinary, and it was all for himself. He resisted
solitude by keeping busy. His activity went way beyond need.
It was an addiction. He built things, made things, fixed things.
He no more wondered at the stars or considered the lilies than
does a dog. He believed in God as Creator and Arbiter, was
reassured to read in one of his Bibles 'Call on Me in the day of
trouble and I will deliver', and then gave sublime attention to
the ordinary. Untroubled by sex, grief, abandonment and the
complexity of life, his twenty-eight years alone on a volcanic
island passed on the level of the husbandry and carpentry of
the day.

Two hundred years after *Robinson Crusoe*'s creation, in a
celebratory essay, the novelist Virginia Woolf described Crusoe's mundanity as a virtue. Defoe, she wrote, kept to his own
perspective:

There are no sunsets and no sunrises; there is no solitude and no soul.
There is, on the contrary, staring us full in the face, nothing but a large
earthenware pot.*

Crusoe's pots were of fireproof clay. He cooked meat and
fish and broth in them. He made clay ovens too, in which he
baked barley loaves, rice cakes and puddings.**

With all his provisions and things, and with God, the parrot and a goat for company, he reflected, as did Selkirk, that he
was happier in isolation than with 'the wicked, cursed, abom-
inable life of earlier days'. He had also retrieved a parcel of
money from the wreck, which prompted him to preach aloud:

*See Virginia Woolf, *The Common Reader* (1925). This essay was first published in *The Times Literary Supplement*, 24 April 1919.
**Defoe had a brick factory in Tilbury in 1694. He knew about firing clay.

O drug, what art thou good for? Thou art not worth to men, no, not the taking off of the ground... Alas! There the nasty, sorry, useless stuff lay; I had no business for it.

What he had instead, were the convenient things that money might purchase. And when, after twenty-three years alone, he found first the print of a bare foot in the sand, and then the man who made it, his dominion was complete:

I made him know his name should be Friday, which was the day I saved his life... I likewise taught him to say master, and then let him know that was to be my name.

Friday was twenty-six, strong, tall and manly. He was olive coloured (not too dark) with black straight hair and fine white teeth. Crusoe made an Englishman of him. He forbade him to eat human beings, tailored linen drawers for him and a jerkin and cap and 'instructed him in the knowledge of the true God':

I told him that the great Maker of all things lived up there, pointing up towards heaven; that He governs the world by the same power and providence by which He had made it; that He was omnipotent, could do everything for us, give everything to us, take everything from us; and thus, by degrees, I opened his eyes. He listened with great attention, and received with pleasure the notion of Jesus Christ being sent to redeem us, and of the manner of making our prayers to God, and His being able to hear us, even into heaven.

So, for Crusoe, he had the company of a slave, God was all consoling, and there were many jobs to be done. Abandonment was not abandonment at all. And as for the scarlet shafts of sunrise, they passed him by.

My Said Wife Frances   1720

WOMEN WERE of passing interest to Selkirk and Crusoe. There was none on their respective islands. Crusoe found his ideal relationship with a male slave. Selkirk made do with goats.

Back in society the terms differed. A man was not a man without a wife. Crusoe married when he returned to England at the age of fifty-eight and after a voyage that had lasted thirty-five years. So as not to slow the narrative, his insignificant wife mothered three children then died, all in the same paragraph.

Nor did Selkirk find a sense of home through marriage. It took a ship, an ocean and a can of flip, to define the work of a day. Women were shadowy creatures, black nymphs, angels, tarts and Jezebels, to be taunted and conquered in the company of men.

In November 1720 he was at the port of Plymouth. He did not find his way home to his 'loveing friend' Sophia Bruce. He signed on as First Mate of a naval warship HMS *Weymouth* which was to make a 'Voyage to Guinea'. For some weeks it was fitted and revictualled: 'Rum and Biskett (20 Baggs)', salt beef, pork, dried peas, oatmeal, butter and fifteen cheeses.

Selkirk drank his flip in a public house in Oarston, a haunt of sailors. Frances Candis, its owner, was as tough a booty seeker as any privateer. He flirted with her, urged on by other drinkers. He told her of the Manila Galleon and that he was worth a thousand pounds.[†]

She would not have sex with him unless they married. He would marry her, he said, before the *Weymouth* sailed. She called him 'very importunate'. He was also very drunk. Asked if he had a wife he 'Solemnly declared he was a Single and an unmarryed Person'. She voiced her doubts, a man of his age and fortune… His drinking friends swore he was free. She knew that drunken sailors were not to be believed.

She claimed she was averse to marrying him but that he insisted. She protested that she could have no life with a man such as he. His ship was leaving within a month. There were the perils and dangers of the seas. She would be a widow before the year was out. She wanted security, so if they married, they must go from the church to her lawyer. Selkirk must make a Will leaving his wages, estate and all he had to her.

The wedding she arranged was on 12 December 1720 in St Andrew's Parish Church in Plymouth. It was a Church of England ceremony. Curate Robert Forster granted the licence. Frances Candis claimed her husband was sober at the time. Her acquaintances – William Warren, John Kimber and Samuel Rhodes witnessed the ceremony.

She took him from the Church to a Plymouth notary. Mr Samuel Bury expressed what he gathered to be Selkirk's intentions in a Will. It was a simpler document than the one lodged with Sophia three years previously. A brief document of betrayal. It made no mention of Katherine Mason, Largo, his family, or Sophia. It simply revoked all former Wills, commended his 'Soul to God that gave it', committed his body to the earth or sea, and bequeathed all his worldly Estate – his Wages due, money, Lands, Tenements, and Estate to his 'wellbeloved wife Frances Selkirk of Oarston & her assignes for ever'.[†]

In the island of his mind it was only a piece of paper, the

price of sex. This woman was no more his wife than Sophia
Bruce. He lived for the opportunism of the moment, without
regard for society's rules. Had his ship docked at Wapping he
might have found his way to Sophia. But it went to Plymouth.

Within days he was heading for the West Coast of Africa,
the chase over, the notch made. Again the wind and the sea
were his rescue. The sea got him away. The *Weymouth*'s task
was to protect merchant ships and rout pirates from the Gulf
of Guinea. Across the familiar ocean was a manly battle to
fight, a journey to be made.[†]

Small Breeze and Fair   1721

IT WAS a doomed voyage. It took him far from The Island's
heart and to the sea's bed. He went to search out pirates who
preyed on English ships and all he found was death. It did not
matter to him to be a turncoat, fighting his own kind. There
was the familiar ghetto of the ship: sparse rations, mutiny and
violence.[†]

The *Weymouth* reached the mouth of the river Gambia in
March 1721. There were gales, haze and great waves. It
seemed an omen of disaster when Alexander Clark wrestling
to reef the sails 'was struck overboard with the saile from the
topsl. yd. and was drowned'. In wind and rain the ship then
grounded in sand. An anchor broke, a cable was damaged. At
high tide there was only fifteen feet of water, at low tide,
seven. For four days the crew heaved and hauled before the
ship was free.

Villagers who lived along this Gold Coast had no reason
to be accommodating to these colonising Whites. Messengers

from the ship who requested water were taken hostage. The ransom demanded for them was of gold and food.

At the rivers and fresh water places, in the dark forests where the men went to cut wood, the dank air was thick with mosquitoes. They were seen as pests and an irritation not as creatures that might kill with a deadly bite. But in June the men of the *Weymouth* began to die: Mr White, Purser, deceased. Mr Peine, Schoolemaster, deceased. Charles Fanshaw, departed this life. John Pritchard, died this day.

The sick could not know their mortal illness was caused by a virus, transmitted by mosquitoes that fed on infected monkeys and then on them. The surgeons blamed the foetid air, the proximity to Negroes. They plied their hopeless craft: phlebotomy and mulled spices.

By late September so many men were dying a makeshift hospital was erected on shore. Twenty Negroes were commandeered without whose help the ship could not be crewed. On 23 October the Governor of Cape Coast Castle informed the *Weymouth*'s Captain, Mungo Herdman, of pirates who had done much damage and taken a Royal African Company ship. The Governor asked for a Muster to be called of men on board who were fit for service. The call was seventy-two: 'Officers, Seamen and Learners, all included'. The following day it was fifty-seven.

Deaths were entered in a daily log, along with laconic comment on the weather, the fixing of a halter around a mutineer's neck and putting him under the Boatswain's command as a Swabber, the taking of men and stores from other ships, the employment of Negroes as a last resort.

In late November Selkirk, too, became unfit for service.

His symptoms were the same as those of other men: burning fever and a shivering chill, headache and muscle pains, vomiting and bloody diarrhoea. He knew that he was dying. It was not the loneliest journey of his life, or the judgement he had feared from The Island's might. He was in the company of men. They offered consolation. As he died he bled from his eyes and mouth.[†]

On 13 December John Barnsley, First Lieutenant of the *Weymouth* wrote in his Log, 'North to northwest. Small Breeze and fair. Took 3 Englishmen out of a Dutch ship and at 8 pm Alexander Selkirk and Wm King died'. The following day it was the turn of William Worthington, Owen Sullivan and Abraham Hudnott.

Wednesday 13 December was a day of small consequence, like the day that preceded and the day that followed. Selkirk's soul was committed to God, his body to the sea, the usual prayers were said. It was not, as he had supposed, The Island's cats he tamed that fed on the meat from his bones, but the fishes of the Atlantic Ocean.

By dying he missed the drama of the pirates' capture: Their trial on board ship. The erection of a scaffold by the shore. The parade of those deemed guilty. The singing of psalms for the sake of their souls. The execution of six men one day, fourteen the next.

In Defoe's novel, Crusoe reached a safe old age. Death for him was another fictional journey. He travelled to heaven in the company of angels, God and Jesus Christ. Selkirk was forty-one when he died. His death was registered in his paybook. There was no other comment on his going. It was silent and unexplained like The Island's night. Money, as ever, signified. The wages owing to him were £35 15s 9d. From this was deducted fifteen shillings for the cost of his seaman's chest and seven and sixpence for fifteen months' medical insurance with the Greenwich hospital.

1722-4 *Wages, Estate and Effects, Goods, Chatells and Credits*

IN HER public house in Plymouth, Frances Selkirk heard of her husband's death at sea. Her thoughts turned to his 'Wages, Estate and Effects', his 'Goods, Chatells and Credits'. She wished to marry a more suitable man, Francis Hall, a tallow chandler.*

She applied to His Majesty's Navy office in Broad Street for Selkirk's wages from the *Weymouth*. Her application was blocked. Sophia Bruce had put in a prior claim. She too said she was Selkirk's widow. She had had his Will proved in the Prerogative Court of Canterbury.** In it he had devised and bequeathed to her his 'Wages Goods Weres Profitts Merchandizes Sume and Sumes of Money Gold Silver Wearing Apparel Bonds Books and any other Thing whatsoever'.

The wives went to lawyers. Sophia protested that she had married Selkirk in March 1717. Her grievance was acute. She claimed the later Will was fraudulent. He had not been free to marry another woman. If he had gone through some spurious wedding ceremony, it was 'when he was much intoxicated with Liquor and non Compos Mentis'.

Frances was determined to get every penny of Selkirk's

*A maker and seller of candles.
**A Prerogative Court was the court of an archbishop for the probate of wills. In 1857 this jurisdiction was transferred to the Court of Probate.

this Sophia had. She maligned her as 'a person of very in-
different character and reputacion'. She married her tallow
chandler and let him know that her previous husband had been
a worthless rogue.

From scrutiny of Sophia's Will, Frances found that her
husband of a week had been richer than she knew. She learned
of the Largo house at Craigie Well, rental income, gold and
silver, bills, bonds and smart money.* She filed an objection at
the Canterbury Court. It was upheld. The Court ruled
Sophia's Will null and void. Its probate was revoked.

Frances then applied to have her own Will proved. Sophia
contested the application and reiterated her case. Frances and
her new husband sued her for refusing to part with Selkirk's
goods, money, estate and effects 'although she hath been severall times thereunto requested in a friendly manner by your
Orators'. She had, they said, 'pieces of Gold, gold rings, and
other particulars and effects of a Considerable Value'.

Sophia was arrested, offered bail of £500 which she could
not raise, and so was imprisoned. While she was in gaol
Frances had her own Will probated. She collected Selkirk's
wages from the *Weymouth* then went up to Largo and claimed
his land, tenements, orchards and house at Craigie Well.

It was not enough. When Sophia was released from gaol
Frances Hall asked her to relinquish all she had in her possession that had once been Selkirk's. But Sophia would not part
with such inheritance as she had: his silver tobacco box and
gold-headed cane, his clothes and sea books and silver-hilted
sword 'and other particulars left in her custody'.

---

*Paid as compensation for disablement or injury while on duty.

Though harassed and goaded, she would not give in. If Selkirk had been married to anyone it was to her. It was she who had offered him consolation for his abandonment on The Island, stayed with him when he was in trouble with the law and lived with him for months on end, not for mere days like this avaricious woman who craved his money, but had cared nothing for his life.

The lawsuits were protracted.† Frances's Petition was heard in the Chancery Courts in January 1723. Selkirk, she said, had sworn he was single when he wooed her. She repeated that she had not wanted to marry him, but he insisted. She gave proof of when and where this marriage took place, its registration and who had witnessed it, and proof of the Will, signed that same day.

She asked that Sophia give account of where and when she had been married, 'in what particular parish Church or place was such pretended marriage solempnized', where was it registered and who had witnessed it. Sophia's Will, she claimed, was a pretence, Selkirk must have been intoxicated and out of his senses if he made it, and anyway it was of a much earlier date, it was null and void, its probate had been revoked.

A year later, on 6 December 1723, Sophia's Petition was heard in Court. The Will in her favour was read out. She claimed she married Selkirk on 4 March 1717. He had then gone to sea with the *Enterprise*. He returned after eight months and stayed with her in London for best part of a year.

This Frances, she said, knew he was already married. She had 'contracted an acquaintance' with Selkirk while he waited for the *Weymouth* to sail. He must have been drunk if he

went through a ceremony with her. She had inveigled him
into it.

Sophia wanted an injunction to prevent Frances and her
new husband taking out further proceedings against her, and
to stop them seizing such assets as she had. They were harass-
ing her. They had caused her to be wrongfully imprisoned and
had deprived her of her husband's estate.

Frances's reply was sworn at Plymouth in February 1724.
She could not say, for she had no proof, whether Selkirk had
ever married Sophia. But when he courted her, Frances, at her
public house in Oarston, he 'swore he was a Single and an Unmarryed Person'. He was not drunk. He knew what he was
doing. Nor had she known of any previous Will. All she knew
was of the Will she had. It revoked all other Wills. It had been
witnessed, registered and probated. He had not made any sub-
sequent Will, gift, or bequest. She and her new husband
wished to keep the forty pounds of Selkirk's wages they had
received and to have it clarified by the Court that they were
entitled to benefit from his Estate and Effects according to the
last Will he had made. They wanted all costs and charges paid
by Sophia.

Sophia lost everything except her belief that she was Mrs
Selkirk. The winter of 1724 was bitterly cold. Among the beg-
ging letters she wrote was one to the Reverend Say in the
Parish of Westminster. She was, she said, 'a person much
reduced to want'. She was 'the widow of Mr Selchrig who
was left four years and four months on the island of John
Ferinanda'. She was sorry to trouble Mr Say. She prayed for
his help. She was a woman of piety and Christian belief. Her
three uncles in Scotland had been ministers.[†]

Selkirk was adept at slipping away from the consequences of a brawl in church, violent assault, false promises or bigamy. Had he survived, in a different port or public house he might have desired some other Frances or Sophia, tempted her with plunder, netted her in a parody of law, notched her like an Island goat.

Selkirk had lived with nothing and with help from no one. The constant of his life had been the call of the sea. It took him to the prospect of riches, to battles he thought manly, to the heart of The Island, to the grave of the ocean.

But at his end all that was focused on was an inventory of booty: rings, clothes, wages and a silver-hilted sword. His legacy was a wrangle for it, claims and counter claims to it, the reduction to poverty of a naïve woman, a litigious justification of greed. It was an echo of the wrangles for plunder on all the voyages he had ever made. It obscured his quest for the Manila galleon, his navigation of the ocean by the sun and stars, his isolation on the implacable Island.

He could not bequeath The Island in words or kind. The Island where he had watched for a sail that only one day came, where his courage was tested, where he had survived abandoned, sustained and protected by its clear water streams, its creatures that foraged, its plants and its trees.

7

THE ISLAND

THE ISLAND

A Magnificent Wilderness   1896

THE ISLAND changed, yet stayed the same. Unfelled sandalwood trees (*Santalum fernandezianum*) laid down their annular
rings. Palms and ferns tangled more densely in valleys and
gulches. Clumps of *Dendroseris micratha* spread tapering leaves
over eroded rocks.

Year on year plunderers thrived. The Island's fur seals
(*Arctocephalus philippii*) were killed for their pelts, massacred
almost to extinction. In 1801 a single ship carried a million skins
to the London market. Only seals on remote rocks and in hidden
bays, survived to regenerate. The huge sea lions (*Otaria jubata*)
were all slaughtered, the sandalwood was felled, the lobsters
were trapped and the whales harpooned.

Visitors to The Island came and went. They praised its
'savage irregular beauty', its woods and verdant valleys and life-

saving streams. The last English privateers wrecked to its shores were from the *Speedwell* in 1719.* For six months The Island was their host.

To spoil The Island as a larder for such men, the Spaniards set loose mastiffs into the valleys. Some goats survived by moving high into the mountain peaks. Most were killed. In a later change of mind, the Spaniards shot the dogs, reintroduced goats, then killed them for their hides.

In 1740 Lord Anson took a naval fleet of English warships to the South Sea. In a voyage of despair men lost their fingers, limbs and lives in freezing gales. Covered in lice 'a peck on each man', they endured starvation, dysentery and scurvy. Out of a crew of two thousand, a third survived to The Island. Their joy was great:

it is scarcely credible with what eagerness and transport we viewed the shore, and with how much impatience we longed for the greens and other refreshments which were then in sight, and particularly for the water... Those only who have endured a long series of thirst can judge of the emotion with which we eyed a large cascade of the most transparent water, which poured itself from a rock near a hundred feet high into the sea, at a small distance from the ship...†

The Spaniards did not want the enemy to view The Island with transport and emotion. They built a deterring fort with stone dungeons and armed with soldiers. A kind of village grew: a dozen huts, a few women and children, eighty cows, pigs and sheep. The fort served too as a prison beyond escape.

War with England ended in 1748. The fort fell to disuse, villagers returned to the mainland, the perception of enemy

---

*They were heading for the Peruvian port of Payta, to attack 'the King of Spain's ships which sail from Lima to Panama with the King's treasure'.

shifted. The Chilean people sought freedom from Spanish colonial rule. Chilean patriots were exiled by the Spaniards to The Island. Consigned to damp caves, they knew nothing of its beneficence.

Castaways, mariners, soldiers, prisoners, hunters, all passed. Waves washed the seals' blood from The Island's bays. In 1823 a British traveller, Maria Graham, walked among the ruins of the fort and dungeons, the abandoned huts, the rusting harpoons and cannon by the shore.* She called The Island a 'magnificent wilderness' and was 'enraptured with the wild beauty of the scenery'. Three herdsmen tending cattle were the only people there. She saw a discarded horse, neglected fields, charred wood from an old fire. She rested among myrtle trees, the mountains rose around her, she felt a shadow of the 'utter loneliness' Selkirk must have known.

A recurring theme of visitors was how The Island might be colonised. A Swiss émigré, Alfred de Rodt, in 1877 put his plans to the Chilean authorities. He would transport sixty people and a thousand cattle to The Island, produce charcoal and export the native palms. He would farm and fish, trap lobsters, kill whales and what were left of the seals.

He was appointed Inspector of Colonisation. Families came from Spain, France, Germany and Switzerland. Their names were Gonzalez, Chamorro, Charpentier, Camacho, Recabarren, Lopez, Schiller. Like other unendangered species they multiplied. When de Rodt died in 1905 The Island had a settlement of 122 human inhabitants. They viewed The Island as theirs.

---

*She published, in 1824, a 'Journal of a Residence in Chili, and a Voyage from Chili to Brazil in the years 1822-3'.

2000 *Isla Robinson Crusoe*

THE ISLAND is now in Chilean territory. De Rodt's colony has grown, but only to 500 people. Their settlement is called *San Juan Bautista* (St John the Baptist). Wooden huts and houses straddle the Great Bay where Selkirk scavenged alone.

The islanders keep Selkirk's memory. In 1966 Blanca Luz Brum, painter, and owner of the *Hostelria Daniel Defoe*, a cluster of shacks by the shore, petitioned the Chilean authorities to change The Island's name from *Mas A Tiera* to *Isla Robinson Crusoe*. She had the tourist trade in mind. The other island in the archipelago, *Mas A Fuera*, was renamed *Isla Alexander Selkirk*, though he never set foot on that unaccommodating rock, which was a danger to avoid.

On *Isla Robinson Crusoe*, in the huts that pass as shops, Crusoe t-shirts and Selkirk wall hangings are sold. A wooden sign directs travellers up a mountain trail to the *Mirador Del Selkirk*, the lonely peak where he searched for a sail.* The cave by the projecting rock in the north-west bay at *Puerto Inglés*, where he never stayed, is known as Selkirk's cave.

The Island's savage terrain and the wide encircling sea, deter *Homo sapiens*. It is possible to link to the World Wide Web, though phone lines are often down. An electricity generator works, on and off. There are one or two cars, no road, newspapers, postman or bank. Credit cards and cheques are not used, or taxes collected. There is a doctor, a dentist, a midwife, but no pharmacy, hospital or vet. Six uniformed *carabinieros* play soccer and collect little children from school on rainy days.

*The Islanders doubt that Selkirk hiked up to the Mirador every day.

Older children go to boarding school in Valparaiso, ferried over in a naval ship in March, then back to The Island in summer for Christmas.

The islanders have a few civic rules. The Municipality, created in 1980, levies rates for water piped from the mountain streams and for maintenance of the pier – on the opposite side of the bay from where Selkirk urged his rescuers to land. A notice in the *Correos*, the post office, by Order of the Municipality, strictly forbids the tethering of animals to the football goalposts. Those who disobey are threatened with a fine.

Islanders refer to mainland Chile as 'the continent'. It seems a world away. In turbulent weather marooned visitors watch the sky. If clear, a small plane flies (courtesy of 'Robinson Crusoe Airlines') to a domestic airport in Chile's capital city, Santiago.* It carries a few people, post, and in season, boxes of lobsters. Its runway is a dirt strip at *El Puente* (the bridge), the only flat bit on The Island, at the low western end where Selkirk went by boat with Dampier to snare goats. Travellers take the same bucketing boat trip from the Great Bay to *Bahia del Padre*, past awesome cliffs, and rocks where fur seals bask and bottle in the sea's spray. There is transit in a decrepit jeep to the airstrip, then a three-hour flight across the ocean.

The islanders live from the sea. Lobsters are their trade. The same endemic creatures (*Jasus frontalis*) Selkirk saw, but then they swarmed the shore and were three feet long. Now they are a dying breed, an endangered species. Year on year the size of the catch and of the lobsters, gets smaller. There is a rule that those caught must measure eleven and a half centimetres, tail to

*Los Cerillos airport.

thorax. Smaller creatures must be returned to the sea. But trade in undersize lobsters remains.* They find their way into *empanadas* and on to the islanders' tables.**

Once a month a supply ship, the *Navarino*, comes from 'the continent' with drums of petrol for the fishing boats, cylinders of gas, fresh vegetables, provisions, building materials and children's toys. In summer it sails on to the other island where, for eight months of the year thirty, lobster fishers live. They look as wild as Selkirk. They come out by boat to meet the ship. It is their lifeline. It takes them letters, cigarettes and *pisco* – a brandy made from grapes. They send gifts home to *Isla Robinson Crusoe*: a box of fish, a blackcurrant bush, a terrified goat.

The lobster factory is in Valparaiso. The *Navarino* returns with its cargo of lobsters. They scrabble and claw in seawater containers nailed with net. A factory official counts them in. Fishermen receive a few hundred pesos for each creature. Smaller lobsters, flung back to the sea, lurch, gulp and head for the life they need. The others, within a day, are taken live by plane to Europe or to the smart restaurants of Santiago.

To save the remaining fur seals, in 1978 they were declared a protected species. Man forbade himself to kill more of them. Some thousands survive around the archipelago. Their voices echo in the bays. Marine biologists observe their feeding patterns, rookeries and hauling grounds and how they treat their young.

Away from protecting eyes there is the same indifference to animal suffering as in Selkirk's day. For meat, a bull is lassoed

*In the 1950s the rule was that lobsters must have reached a length of 15.5 cms, tail to thorax, before they could be eaten. This was reduced to 13 cms and in 2000, 11 cms.
**Empanadas are a sort of pastie.

then dragged down from the hills. It bellows and is beaten with sticks on its long reluctant journey. The men's hands bleed as they pull it by a rope from its horns. Dogs yelp and snap at its legs. It arrives defeated at the crude abattoir. It is tethered to the gnarled root of a tree for its last night. In its eyes are depression, or perhaps rage.

Next morning the smell of rendered fat comes from the abattoir. Lumps of hacked meat are pushed from it in a barrow. Notices are soon scrawled on cardboard in windows: *Hoy. Empanadas con carne.**

Away from such activity are the still mountains and fissured cliffs, the deep forests, dense luma and chonta, the tree ferns and grasses. The Island has its unobserved life, its own laws. The fire that formed it four million years past still burns. The wind curls through the valleys. Seisms and tsunamis warn. Waves hurl high from a calm sea catching rainbows of sunlight in their spray.

A Worldwide Reserve of the Biosphere   2000

THE ISLAND'S mountains, valleys and gulches are now measured and mapped. With the same passion for inventory shown by the privateers, its birds, snails, lichens, algae, psocoptera, palms and peperomias, bryophytes and gymnospheres, are counted, classified, named and sorted. Sixty per cent of its plants are unique to it. There are 131 kinds of moss and 20 sorts of fern.

In 1935 it was declared a national park. This was in large part a response to the work of a Swedish botanist, Carl Skottsberg.[†] It intrigued him that life forms that would die at the touch of

---

*Today there are meat pasties.

seawater, that preceded man by a million years, had their home on it, that their ancestors passed uninjured over vast stretches of ocean, or survived on this leftover fragment of unsubmerged land. He saw The Island as a unique ecosystem, a world in microcosm, to be protected and preserved.

But the islanders, like Crusoe, saw it as their estate. For decades they lived without rules or prohibitions. They felled the endemic palms to build their boats and houses, planted blackberry which spread like fire and choked the native plants, and they imported sheep, cattle and goats, which grazed the vegetation and eroded the soil.

In 1969 Carlos Munoz Pizzaro gave a paper to the Academy of Science in Chile. He advocated that boundaries for the park be set, that no building or motor vehicles be allowed in it, that cattle, rats, rabbits, coati (*Nasua nasua* – brought from Uraguay) and blackberry be eradicated and the primary forest restored.

Four years later CONAF, the Chilean Forestry Commission, took on responsibility for The Island.* Their aim was to preserve it and to restore its endangered species. An administrator and park wardens arrived. Islanders were forbidden to fell trees or take plants. They resented the intrusion. They viewed the wardens as interlopers, were abusive to them and even violent.

To conservationists The Island's significance went beyond national territory or local need. In microcosm they saw the world's problems of land erosion, overfishing, the destruction of species that cannot be reborn, the breakdown of the interdependence of living things.

In 1977 UNESCO declared The Island a Worldwide Reserve

---

*Corporacion Nacional Forestal.

of the Biosphere. The intention was to preserve its generic species and conserve its ecosystem. Holland gave a grant of two and a half million dollars, Czechoslovakia sent germinating chambers, greenhouses and chemicals to kill the blackberry. Chile paid the salaries of CONAF employees. The Island's boundaries were set: 164 yards up from the village the World-wide Reserve began. The islanders were allotted 1000 acres of land around San Juan Bautista and the airstrip. The Reserve claimed the rest of the archipelago: 24,000 acres on the two islands and the islet of Santa Clara.

Year on year the primary forest is extended from high to low altitude. Erosion of the soil is arrested with dams. Cattle and goats may only graze on certain hills, rabbits are shot and money paid for their tails. In the conditions they need, the white flowering shrub *Dendroseris neriifolia* is germinated, cultivated and protectively replanted, so are spiky leaved *Ochagavia elegans*, yellow flowering *Robinsonia thurifera*, the *Yunquea tenzii*, the myrtle *Ugni selkirkii*, white and red campanulae, the scarce mauve orchid *Herbetia lahue*.[†] The climate favours regeneration. There is plenty of sunshine and rain and no hard winter. Three hundred plants are reintroduced each day in the conditions they need. A centre has been built to teach tourists, islanders and children about The Island's flora and fauna, its geology and history.

Man, more pestilential than the rat or rabbit, is banned from living in the Reserve. Islanders are accorded what they are deemed to need. CONAF has planted fast-growing cypress and eucalyptus trees for wood for their boats and houses. They are told that 'ecotourism' will bring money. They are employed as park wardens. Young men replant the forests, poison the blackberry and rats and shoot the goats and rabbits.

The scheme has problems. The Island is not entire of itself. Its seas are plundered, its climate altered. When all the rabbits are killed, so too is the food supply of The Island's buzzards (*Buteo polyosoma exul*). When the blackberry is all poisoned, the soil erodes, thrushes are denied their favourite food and the islanders a particular kind of pie. Like Crusoe's God, CONAF decides what will live and what will die. There is an intangibility in wanting to keep what once was there. The Island might have the last say. Nasturtiums, poppies and amaryllis from South America and South Africa are unwelcome guests. It was not the fault of the rabbits (*Oryctolagus cuniculus*) that they arrived with such a capacity to reproduce and such voracious appetites, or that they erode the soil by digging burrows. They, like the cattle, goats, rats, dogs and cats, were transported on ships, then abandoned on The Island to adapt as they could.

Man's late dream is of more than Crusoe's market garden. It is of an image of the kind of garden the world might have been. Selkirk was a rough man and as bad and careless as others, but The Island was perforce his world. Though he longed to escape it, though he searched each day for the sail of rescue, he depended on it and was sustained by it. Three hundred years on, it is man's privilege to leave the seals to graze, arrest erosion, restore the sandalwood trees, extend the forest, guard, protect and preserve the endemic species that net living creatures to their past, that net us all together.* In such intervention there is a dream beyond the pursuit of gold. There is deference to The Island's grace and to a marooned man's heart.

---

*Two sandalwood trees have escaped extinction high in the primary forest on the Yunque mountain. Perhaps from these two trees, more will grow.

ENDNOTES

AND

INDEX

ENDNOTES

Half title: Alfred, Lord Tennyson wrote *Enoch Arden* in the winter of 1861. It is a long narrative poem about lovers, a sea voyage, a desert island and a tragic homecoming.

2. THE JOURNEY

page number

23 An oil portrait of Dampier, c. 1698, by Thomas Murray, is now in the National Portrait Gallery, London. Hans Sloane, Secretary to the Royal Society, commissioned it. For biographical information see Anton Gill, *The Devil's Mariner* (1997); B.M.H. Rogers, 'Dampier's Debts' and 'Dampier's Voyage of 1703', *Mariner's Mirror*, 25 (1924); Joseph Shipman, *William Dampier: Seaman-Scientist* (1962); Glyn Williams, *The Great South Sea* (1997).

23 See (and following) Dampier's published journals: *A New Voyage Round the World* (1697); *A Collection of Voyages* I-IV (1729) and John Masefield (ed.), *Dampier's Voyages* (1906).

25 See Glyn Williams, *The Prize of All the Oceans* (1999), an account of Lord Anson's quest for the Manila galleon.

27 See William Dampier, *Voyages and Descriptions*, vol. II (1699).

30 Papers relating to Dampier's court martial in 1702 are in the Public Record Office, London (Adm.I/1692).

30 Dampier to the Admiralty. Abridged in John Masefield (ed.), *Dampier's Voyages*, (vol. II).

30 Meangis is one of the remote Sangihe and Talaud islands, in the Celebes Sea, between Sulawesi and the Philippine island of Mindanao.

31 From Dampier's manuscript journal (Sloane MS 3236 f.203v). Hans Sloane acquired this and many other buccaneers' journals. They now form the Sloane Collection at the British Library.

32 This poster, with similar advertisements, is in the Manuscripts collection in the British Library (552 d.18 (2)).

32   See *Prince Giolo Son of the King of Moangis or Gilolo: Lying Under the Equator in Long. of 152 Dig. 30 Min. a Fruitful Island Abounding with Rich Spices and Other Valuable Commodities*(1692), and Thomas Hyde, *An Account of the Famous Prince Giolo* (1692).

33   Basil Ringrose, *Bucaniers* II, British Library (Sloane MS 48 f.86).

34   Dampier, *A New Voyage Round the World*.

34   See *Bucaniers* II, British Library (Sloane MS 48 f.87); Glyn Williams, *The Great South Sea*; and Burg, B.R., *Sodomy and the Pirate Tradition* (1984).

36   See John Masefield (ed.), *Dampier's Voyages* (vol. I).

37   Translated in R. L. Woodward, *Robinson Crusoe's Island: A History of the Juan Fernandez Islands* (1969).

39   See 'Letters and Papers Relating to the Voyage of the *St George*', in John Masefield (ed.), Dampier's *Voyages* (vol. II); and B.M.H.Rogers, 'Dampier's Voyage of 1703', *Mariner's Mirror*, 15 (1924).

40   Masefield, op. cit.

40   See the Burney Collection of early newspapers in the British Library

42   For details of eighteenth-century shipboard life see N.A.M. Rodger, *The Wooden World* (1988).

42   A letter from William Price to Edward Southwell, 10 July 1703. Quoted in Anton Gill, *The Devil's Mariner* (1997).

42   There is disagreement over the size of the *Cinque Ports*. This description is taken from its Letter of Marque in the Public Record Office (HCA 26/18). William Funnell in his *Voyage Round the World* (1707) describes it as weighing 90 tons, with 20 guns and 63 men.

42   For speculation on Selkirk's rank, see C.D.Lee, 'Alexander Selkirk and the Last Voyage of the *Cinque Ports Galley*', *Mariner's Mirror*, 73 (1987).

43   John Howell, Selkirk's first biographer, gleaned such anecdotal information from a great-grand-nephew of Selkirk. See *The Life and Adventures of Alexander Selkirk* (1829).

44   G.H. Healey (ed.), *The Letters of Daniel Defoe* (1955).

44   See Largo Parish Records; R.L.Mergoz, *The Real Robinson Crusoe* (1939); and A.S.Cunningham, 'Upper Largo, Lower Largo, Lundin Links and Newburn' (undated).

45   John Prebble, *The Darien Disaster* (1968).

45 William Paterson, 'A Proposal to Plant a Colony in Darien' (1701). And see G.P.Insh, *The Company of Scotland Trading to Africa and the Indies* (1932).

47 Lionel Wafer, *A New Voyage and Description of the Isthmus of America* (Hakluyt Society, 1934).

49 See 'Upper Largo, Lower Largo, Lundin Links and Newburn'.

50 See his *Voyage Round the World* (1707).

51 As well as 'The South Sea Waggoner', Selkirk would have referred to Mount and Page, 'New Sea Atlas' (1702); by Captain Greenvile Collins (Hydrographer in Ordinary to the King and Queen's most Excellent Majesties), 'Great Britain's Coasting Pilot' (1693) and John Seller, 'Southern Navigation' (1703). Originals of these charts and pilot books are in the National Maritime Museum, London.

51 See Derek Howse, 'Navigation and Astronomy in the Voyages' in *Background to Discovery: Pacific Exploration from Dampier to Cook* (1990).

52 Op. cit. And see Dava Sobel, *Longitude* (1996).

53 Funnell, *A Voyage Round the World*.

53 John Welbe's accusations and Dampier's 'vindication' of these, are included in John Masefield (ed.), *Dampier's Voyages* (vol. II). And see dusty cardboard boxes of unsorted contemporary documents about the voyage, stained with seawater and sprinkled with sand, in Chancery 104/160, in the Public Record Office, London.

54 Funnell, *A Voyage Round the World*. And following.

55 The Wellcome Institute Library, London, has an archive on the history of medicine at sea. For ghoulish detail see John Woodall, *The Surgeon's Mate* (1617).

56 See Francis E. Cuppage, *James Cook and the Conquest of Scurvy* (1994), and J.J.Keevil, *Medicine and the Navy* (1958).

58 Funnell, *A Voyage Round the World*.

59 John Welbe, 'An Answer to Captain Dampier's Vindication of his Voyage to the South Seas in the Ship *St George*', in John Masefield (ed.), *Dampier's Voyages*, (vol. II).

59 Selkirk's criticisms of the voyage are in a sworn Deposition, dated 10 July 1712, Chancery 24/1321, Public Record Office.

61 See Funnell, *A Voyage Round the World*; B.M.H.Rogers, 'Dampier's Voyage of 1703'; Welbe's 'Answer to Captain Dampier's Vindication'; and Selkirk's Deposition.

62 Eighteenth-century mariners described The Island in their published books. They showed no sparkle in their choice of titles for these journals. As well as Funnell's *Voyage Round the World,* see Woodes Rogers, *A Cruising Voyage Round the World* (1712); Edward Cooke, *A Voyage to the South Sea and Round the World* (1712); George Shelvocke, *A Voyage Round the World by Way of the Great South Sea* (1726); and George Anson, *A Voyage Round the World* (1748).

62 See Funnell, *A Voyage Round the World*. And following.

65 John Welbe, *An Answer to Captain Dampier's Vindication*. Depositions corroborating Welbe's account of Dampier's behaviour were given in 1712 in the Chancery Courts by Selkirk, William Sheltram and Ralph Clift. Public Record Office (Chancery 24/1321).

65 Sheltram's Deposition.

66 Funnell, *A Voyage Round the World*.

67 John Woodall, *The Surgeon's Mate* (1617). And see John Kirkup's introduction and appendix to a facsimile of this (1978).

68 Welbe's 'Answer' to Dampier's 'Vindication'.

69 See Clift's Deposition, and those of Selkirk and Sheltram.

71 Welbe's 'Answer' to Dampier's 'Vindication'.

73 Dampier's 'Vindication'.

74 Welbe's 'Answer', and the Depositions of Selkirk, Sheltram and Clift.

77 See Selkirk's Deposition.

3. THE ARRIVAL

85 For contemporary accounts of Selkirk on The Island, see Woodes Rogers, *A Cruising Voyage Round the World* (1712); Edward Cooke, *A Voyage to the South Sea and Round the World* (1712); and an article by Richard Steele in the *Englishman* (26), 1-3 December, 1713.

90 Steele, the *Englishman*, December 1713.

93 See John Howell, *Alexander Selkirk* (1829); Edward Cooke, *A Voyage to the South Sea*; Woodes Rogers, *Cruising Voyage*; Richard Steele, the *Englishman*.

94 The poet William Cowper (1731-1800) in 1782 wrote *Verses supposed to be written by Alexander Selkirk, during his solitary abode in the island of Juan Fernandez:*

>   I am monarch of all I survey,
>   My right there is none to dispute,
>   From the centre all round to the sea,
>   I am lord of the fowl and the brute.
>   O solitude! Where are the charms
>   That sages have seen in thy face?
>   Better dwell in the midst of alarms,
>   Than reign in this horrible place.
>   *Etcetera.*

94 Woodes Rogers, *A Cruising Voyage*.
94 Steele, the *Englishman*.
94 Deposition, 1712.

95 C.D.Lee, 'Alexander Selkirk and the Cinque Ports Galley', *Mariner's Mirror*, 73 (1987).

97 See John Masefield (ed.), *Dampier's Voyages* (Vol. II); and the Depositions of Selkirk, Clift and Sheltram.

99 Funnell, *A Voyage Round the World*.

100 Woodes Rogers, *A Cruising Voyage*.
100 Ibid.

102 Woodes Rogers, *A Cruising Voyage*

103 See J.M.Coetzee, *Foe* (1986); Pat Rogers, *Robinson Crusoe* (1979); Derek Walcott, *The Castaway and Other Poems* (1965).

105 Nicolaus Copernicus, *De Revolutionibus Orbium Coelestium* (1543). Before his time the Earth was thought to be at rest, with the Sun, Planets and Stars circling round it.
105 See Welbe's 'Answer', Dampier's 'Vindication' and Funnell's *Voyage*.

106 B.M.H.Rogers, 'Dampier's Voyage of 1703'.

107 Dampier's 'Vindication'.

109 See the Depositions of Selkirk, Clift and Sheltram, and the Chancery Papers 104/160 in the Public Record Office.

4. THE RESCUE

115 For source material for this 1708 voyage, see the published journals of Woodes Rogers and Edward Cooke; David J. Starkey, *British Privateering Enterprise* (1990); Glyn Williams, *The Great South Sea* (1997); B.M.H.Rogers, 'Woodes Rogers's Privateering Voyage of 1708-11', *Mariner's Mirror* 19 (1928).

116 Chancery 104/160, Public Record Office.

117 HCA 26/18, Public Record Office.

118 Chancery 104/160, Public Record Office.

119 Chancery 104/16, Public Record Office.
119 Woodes Rogers, *A Cruising Voyage*. And following.

130 Woodes Rogers to owners, February 1708. Chancery 104/160, Public Record Office.
130 Woodes Rogers, *A Cruising Voyage*.

133 Edward Cooke, *A Voyage to the South Sea*.

134 Woodes Rogers, *A Cruising Voyage*.
134 Edward Cooke, *A Voyage to the South Sea*.

135 Woodes Rogers, *A Cruising Voyage*.

136 Woodes Rogers, *A Cruising Voyage*; Edward Cooke, *A Voyage to the South Sea*; Bryan Little, *Crusoe's Captain: Being the Life of Woodes Rogers, Seaman, Trader, Colonial Governor* (1960).
136 Woodes Rogers, *A Cruising Voyage*. And following.

138 See Chancery 104/160 and 104/61, Public Record Office.

141 Vanbrugh in a letter to the Bristol owners, 11 December 1710. Chancery 104/160, Public Record Office.
141 Woodes Rogers, *A Cruising Voyage*.

143 Richard Hitchman in a statement to Dr Dover, undated, Chancery 104/61, Public Record Office.

144 Woodes Rogers, *A Cruising Voyage*.

145 Charles Darwin, *The Origin of Species by Means of Natural Selection* (1859); Nora Barlow (ed.), *Charles Darwin's Diary of the Voyage of HMS Beagle* (1933).

146 See the entry in Captain Courtney's Committee Book for 29 August 1709. Chancery 104/36 (part 2), Public Record Office.

146 Woodes Rogers, *A Cruising Voyage*; Edward Cooke, *A Voyage to the South Sea*; Bryan Little, *Crusoe's Captain*.

147 Woodes Rogers, *A Cruising Voyage*. And following.

149 Edward Cooke, *A Voyage to the South Sea*; Bryan Little, *Crusoe's Captain*.

150 Woodes Rogers, *A Cruising Voyage*; Edward Cooke, *A Voyage to the South Sea*. And following.

152 Woodes Rogers to Owners, 25 July 1710, Chancery 104/160, Public Record Office.

152 Thomas Dover to Owners, 11 February 1711, Chancery 104/60, Public Record Office.

155 Woodes Rogers to Owners, 25 July 1710, Chancery 104/160, Public Record Office.

155 Woodes Rogers, *A Cruising Voyage*. And see Bryan Little, *Crusoe's Captain*.

156 See Woodes Rogers, 'An Abstract of the Most Remarkable Transactions', 6 February 1711; and Letters to Owners from Stephen Courtney, Edward Cooke, Thomas Dover and Woodes Rogers, all in Chancery 104/160, Public Record Office.

156 Woodes Rogers to Owners, 25 July 1710, Chancery 104/160, Public Record Office.

157 See the ships' Committee Books, parts one and two, Chancery 104/36, Public Record Office.

158 Thomas Dover to Owners, 11 February 1711, Chancery 104/60, Public Record Office.

159 James Hollidge, merchant and Mayor of Bristol, to Owners, 18 August 1711, Chancery 104/160, Public Record Office.

159 See D/19 and E/13, 1711, in the Oriental and India Office Collection at the British Library.

160 See the Burney Collection of Early Newspapers in the British Library.

5. LONDON SCRIBBLERS

163 William Funnell, *A Voyage Round the World*.

163 Dampier's Vindication.

166 Cooke surmised that the 'certain officer' was Dampier. But it was
Stradling that Selkirk loathed.

167 Woodes Rogers, *A Cruising Voyage*; and see G.E. Manwaring's introduction to a reprint of this in 1928.

169 See George A. Aitken, *The Life of Richard Steele* (1889).

170 See the *Post-Boy*, October 29-31, 1713.

174 See East India Company correspondence E1/3 and D/92, Oriental and
India Office Library Collection, British Library, and Glyn Williams,
The Great South Sea (1997).

176 (C24/1321 pt. 1) Public Record Office.

177 Ibid.

178 *Review*, no. 68, 30 August 1711.

179 Correspondence concerning proposals for this South Sea project is in
Add MS 28, 140, British Library. And see John E. Flint & Glyndwr
Williams, *Perspectives of Empire* (1973).

179 Add MSS 25, 494, British Library.

180 W.H.Hart came across this indictment while researching eighteenth-
century Queen's Bench records. See *Notes and Queries*, 30 March 1861.

6. HOME

183 This anecdote was told to Selkirk's first biographer, John Howell, by a
great-grand-nephew of Selkirk's. See *The Life and Adventures of Alexander Selkirk* (1829).

184 John Howell, *The Life and Adventures of Alexander Selkirk*.

185 See R.L. Megroz, *The Real Robinson Crusoe* (1939).

185 See Henry Cadwallader Adams, *The Original Robinson Crusoe* (1877).

186 See Bryan Little, *Crusoe's Captain*.

186 See the Log Books of the *Enterprise* and *Weymouth*, Admiralty Records 52/316, Public Record Office.

186 This will was published in the *Scots Magazine,* vol.67 (1805).

189 See Thomas Wright, *The Life of Daniel Defoe* (1894); James Sutherland, *Defoe* (1937); Pat Rogers, *Robinson Crusoe* (1979).

195 The petitions of Frances Candis and Sophia Bruce are in Chancery II/52/31 and Chancery II/297/61 (1714-58), Public Record Office.

196 Selkirk's will of 1720 is also in the Public Record Office.

197 The logbooks of the *Weymouth* are in Admiralty 4/53 and Ad. Rec. 52/316 in the Public Record Office .

197 For the paybooks of the *Weymouth* see Admiralty 33/308 in the National Maritime Museum.

199 See J.J. Keevil, *Medicine and the Navy* (1958).

202 See Chancery II/52/31 and 297/61 in the Public Record Office.

203 See 'The Say Papers' in *Monthly Repository,* 1810. And see R.L. Megroz, *The Real Robinson Crusoe.*

7. THE ISLAND

208 See Richard Walter, *Anson's Voyage Round the World* (1928); and Glyn Williams, *The Prize of All the Oceans* (1999).

213 See Carl Skottsberg (1880-1963), *The Natural History of Juan Fernandez* (1922).

215 See Philippe Danton, *Les Iles de Robinson* (Paris 1999).

INDEX

East India Company, 159, 174

Elizabeth I, Queen of England, 25

Englishman (journal), 170–71 & n

Enterprise, HMS, 186–7, 202

Essex, HMS, 160

Estcourt, Thomas: backs 1703 expedition, 23–4, 26, 38; death, 109; heirs, 175

Evelyn, John, 30

Falkland Islands, 122

Fame (ship), 39

fardelas (seabirds), 19, 37

Fernandez, Don Juan, 36

fish, 18, 54–5, 63

flamingos, 28

Forster, Revd Robert, 196

France: Dampier attacks merchantmen, 64–6; profits in South Seas, 116; ships in South Seas, 131; threat to *Batchelor* on voyage to Britain, 158

Frye, Edward, 145–6, 166

Frye, Robert, 125, 127

Funnell, William: sails with Dampier as Second Mate, 39; on conditions aboard *St George*, 50, 57; on Madeira, 52; on Cape Verde Islanders, 53; criticises Dampier's navigation, 61; complains of losing Spanish ship, 69; in attack on Santa Maria, 71, 73; takes command of *Assumsion*, 74; Selkirk hopes for rescue by, 88; on shipworm damage, 96; in fight with Spanish warship, 97; deserts Dampier, 106; returns home, 108; publishes account blaming Dampier, 163

Galapagos Islands, 28, 142–5

galleons: defined, 26n

Gallera (island), 97

Gallo (island), 70

Gambia, river, 197

George, Prince of Denmark, 117

Giolo, Prince of Meangis, 30–32

goats, prevalence on Island, 18, 37–8, 208; as food, 35; Selkirk hunts, eats and uses, 89, 92, 100–102, 130–31, 192, 195; Selkirk husbands, 93–4; in *Robinson Crusoe*, 192

God: Selkirk's faith in, 90, 169; Crusoe on, 194

Godolphin, Mary, 190

Godolphin, Sidney, 1st Earl of, 39

Gold Coast, 197–8

Goldney, Thomas, 116

Gorgona Island, 98, 142

Graham, Maria, 209 & n

Guam, 108, 147, 154

Guayaquil, 24, 96, 132; attacked and plundered, 134–41

Guinea, Gulf of, 197–8

Hack, William, 24n

Halifax, 1st Earl of *see* Montagu, Charles

Hall, Francis, 200

Hardy, Rear-Admiral Sir Thomas, 160

Harley, Sir Robert *see* Oxford, 1st Earl of

Harrison, John, 52

Hatley, Simon, 144 & n

Havre de Grace (French ship) *see* *Marquess*

Herdman, Captain Mungo, 198

Hill, James, 39, 50

Hollidge, James, 159

Hopeful Binning (ship), 48

hummingbirds, 19, 37, 63, 91, 111

Huxford, Samuel, 39, 50, 53–4, 84